Media

Polity's *Why It Matters* series

In these short and lively books, world-leading thinkers make the case for the importance of their subjects and aim to inspire a new generation of students.

Helen Beebee & Michael Rush, *Philosophy*
Nick Couldry, *Media*
Robert Eaglestone, *Literature*
Andrew Gamble, *Politics*
Lynn Hunt, *History*
Tim Ingold, *Anthropology*
Neville Morley, *Classics*
Alexander B. Murphy, *Geography*
Geoffrey K. Pullum, *Linguistics*
Graham Ward, *Theology and Religion*

Nick Couldry

Media

Why It Matters

polity

The right of Nick Couldry to be identified as Author of this Work has been asserted in
accordance with the UK Copyright, Designs and Patents Act 1988.

First published in 2020 by Polity Press

Polity Press
65 Bridge Street
Cambridge CB2 1UR, UK

Polity Press
101 Station Landing
Suite 300
Medford, MA 02155, USA

ISBN-13: 978-1-5095-1514-1
ISBN-13: 978-1-5095-1515-8 (pb)

A catalogue record for this book is available from the British Library.

Library of Congress Cataloging-in-Publication Data

Names: Couldry, Nick, author.
Title: Media : why it matters / Nick Couldry.
Description: Cambridge, UK ; Medford, MA : Polity, 2019. | Series: Why it
    matters | Includes bibliographical references. | Summary: "The media
    plays a massive role in shaping the world as we see it. Couldry explains
    the significance of five core dimensions of media, and shows that
    understanding these dynamics is a vital skill that every person needs in
    the digital age, when the fate of our political worlds and social
    environment may rest on how we communicate with each other"-- Provided
    by publisher.
Identifiers: LCCN 2019020466 (print) | LCCN 2019981525 (ebook) | ISBN
    9781509515141 (hardback) | ISBN 9781509515158 (paperback) | ISBN
    9781509515189 (epub)
Subjects: LCSH: Mass media.
Classification: LCC P90 .C689 2019 (print) | LCC P90 (ebook) | DDC
    302.23--dc23
LC record available at https://lccn.loc.gov/2019020466
LC ebook record available at https://lccn.loc.gov/2019981525

Typeset in 11 on 15 Sabon by Servis Filmsetting Ltd, Stockport, Cheshire
Printed and bound in the UK by CPI Group (UK) Ltd, Croydon

For further information on Polity, visit our website: politybooks.com

To Chris, Imogen, and Will

Contents

Acknowledgements

This book was written between June 2018 and June 2019, in a period of considerable turbulence and rising controversy in media, politics and society in Brazil, Hungary, India, the UK, the USA, Venezuela, and many other places. Rather than bracket out that context, I have tried to reflect it.

Thanks to Pascal Porcheron of Polity for his invitation in 2016 to write a book in Polity's *Why It Matters* series, his patience with a slower schedule than originally planned, and his perceptive editorial input. Thanks to Ellen MacDonald-Kramer for her support too and to Justin Dyer for a sharp and sensitive copy-edit of the manuscript.

I also want to thank various institutions and people without whom the book, once committed, could never have been written or completed. In terms of institutions, thanks to the Department of

Acknowledgements

Media and Communications at the London School of Economics and Political Science, which granted the sabbatical during which this book was written; and thanks to the Berkman Klein Center for Internet and Society at Harvard University and MIT's Comparative Media Studies programme for being congenial homes in autumn 2018. Turning to people, particular thanks to my niece Isobel Edwards for carefully reading an earlier draft and reassuring me that I had made at least some progress in shedding the jargon and unnecessary detail that often gets in the way of academic writing. And thanks to Yongchan Kim for advice about media in Korean history; to Kim Schrøder for alerting me to the original version of the Stuart Hall research paper discussed in Chapter 2; and to Sonia Livingstone and Rafał Zaborowski for conversations over a number of years about the 'media deprivation' exercise as performed in their Media Audiences course at the LSE. Many thanks also to João Vieira-Magalhães for research assistance and, as ever, excellent help on many matters of detail. Thanks to three anonymous reviewers for Polity for helpful and constructive comments that helped me to produce a better version. And heartfelt thanks to Louise Edwards not just for commenting on the manuscript, but even more importantly for

Acknowledgements

tolerating my frequent distractions and absences during much of this book's writing and for her clarity, as always, in grasping what really matters. The faults that remain are my responsibility.

I dedicate this book to Chris Powell, Imogen Crarer, and Will Crarer. In their world, media will surely matter even more than in mine – whether for good or ill, we must wait and see.

Nick Couldry
Islip, near Oxford
June 2019

Introduction

Imagine your life without media.

This is a standard exercise in media classes, but it's hard to put into practice, even for a day. It's a little like being forced to navigate across a room completely blindfolded. And yet imagining your daily routine without media involves more than just imagining the lack of a sense. It means imagining a world that is, like ours, organized around media and the assumption we all have access to media, where suddenly *you* don't hold the resource of media in your hand.

What makes the 'media deprivation' exercise hard is the act of *social* imagination it requires. We have become used to organizing social life – and wider society – *through* what we do with media. Operating on a different basis, even for a day, requires us to imagine the routines of a society different from the one we live in.

Introduction

The difficulty of sustaining the media deprivation exercise is an example of a problem identified sixty years ago by the biologist Gregory Bateson. Bateson called this 'the double bind': even if we choose *not* to communicate, we end up communicating something, just by that abstinence. In a similar way, even withdrawing from all our systems for communicating through media sends a message. That's why students doing the media deprivation exercise often have to stop: their parents are anxiously calling round to ask what's wrong with them. It is as if, by *not* communicating, they were sending a message.

Media matter in our world, and in a particular way. Having access to certain information flows according to particular rhythms matters for whether contemporary societies are characterized by order or chaos; it affects what sort of social order is possible. These are flows not just of information, but maybe of other resources too: visibility, the possibility to connect, and some control over what images and information reach us. Social order depends today on a media order, which makes certain demands of us: the requirement to be connected and to follow what our 'networks' are doing; the requirement to be tracked by platforms.

Yet having access to media means something different to different people. The global businessperson with three phones and numerous other connected devices has a very different relation to media from the Chinese migrant worker who works in the factory that makes those devices but may only share a phone with family or friends, or the Filipino micropayment worker who, far from sight, 'cleans' social media platforms of shocking material, or the UK contract nurse who relies on a smartphone app to access her next job.

Even the types of things you might mean when you talk about your experiences of media could vary hugely. You might mean your personal collection of photos, music tracks, vlogs, and podcasts, and how you keep track of them all. You might mean a live television broadcast (royal ceremony or major football game) and your experience of chatting about it with friends via your mobile phone as the broadcast went on. You might mean sending to someone on the other side of the world a favourite image, song, or TV programme via a weblink, or sending her money via a payment system. Or you might have in mind the version of normal life that the mainstream news media presents, and the battles of some, yourself included, to make a different reality visible. Such battles can take a very practical form: for example, filming an act of violence on the street right in front of you and posting it online where others can see it and protest about it. 'Media' – our experience of media – spans everything from daily habits of media use to the social reality that is presented by media. As media transmission becomes embedded in the most ordinary of objects, 'media' can even include how your smart TV (refrigerator, watch, whatever) tracks your interactions with it, whether you like it or not.

Is there a common definition of the term 'media' that underlies all this variety? The working definition of 'media' that we will adopt in this book is as follows: *technologies that are able regularly and reliably to transmit or preserve meanings across space and time* (from a simple 'yes' or 'no' to the most elaborate textual creation, whether a Shakespeare play or a multi-series television drama). In the age of digital media, media inevitably involve computing power of some sort. Such power is embedded in almost all media technologies (from phones to tablets to large computer servers). The complexity of the category 'media' is already clear.

There's another complexity too that we have to face if we adopt even this basic definition of 'media'. For in thinking about media, we must think across a number of dimensions. There is the technology of transmission itself, but there is also the content that is transmitted and, over the long term, stored. There are the industries and organizations that produce that technology and that content. And, at the other end of the media process, there are the people and organizations that use media devices, make sense of the contents sent to them, or send their own messages through media platforms.

And, as the difficulty of performing the media deprivation exercise teaches us, there is the question of what difference all these many aspects of media make to the societies in which we live. In thinking about media, therefore, the challenge is to think about media as a dimension of how contemporary life *as a whole* is shaped; how today's societies find their form.

In surveying what it might mean to study and think about media, this book will inevitably make selections. I won't spend much time on the details of media industries, even though they are important places in which to work and the economics that drives them is fascinating. I also won't spend much time on the details of how media messages might influence us to believe certain things, or at least think about certain things. If, after reading this book, you decide you want to study media further, you will soon find the large body of research on these topics which has influenced the story about media that I tell here.

Introduction

Instead I have chosen a different way into media as a subject. I will look at media's role in how we experience the world, and the work media do in constructing the world in which we live. This choice has an impact on the language I will use in this book. Media are tools for telling back to us the story of our world. In that sense, media stand in for 'everything'. And yet media are also many things, and many types of thing (institutions, types of content interfaces, audiences). That's probably why, in some versions of English, the noun 'media' is treated as both singular and plural. I have already relied on that ambiguity: compare the book's title – *Media: Why* It *Matters* – to sentences in this introduction where the word 'media' takes a plural verb. If that, for your version of English, sounds strange, I can only apologize. But this grammatical instability of the word 'media' in some versions of English is no accident. It captures how a complex and often conflicted set of institutions, techniques, and mechanisms for connecting and representing human beings (which we call 'media') can build *a* landscape, *a* world. That process – of making worlds *through* media and our uses of media – is the topic of this book.

This way of thinking about media – and media's importance to the type of world we live in – is no substitute for studying history, politics, or economics. But it is an approach to the world (and media) that can enrich your thinking whether you are an economist or historian, sociologist or scientist, artist or lawyer. So much so that, over the past four decades, large numbers of students and researchers have decided it is worth studying as a specialism in its own right. By 'studying', I have in mind the great Brazilian educator Paulo Freire's definition of study as 'thinking about experience'. 'Thinking about experience', Freire wrote, 'is the best way to think accurately.'[1] All of us have plenty of experience of media. Studying media, then, in spite of the media's own caricatures, at times, of 'media studies', is hardly trivial. It means drawing on this experience to think seriously about the complexity and depth of how media are changing the societies and world we live in.

Societies are not like blocks of stone fallen from the sky. It is the human members of societies, and the institutions and infrastructures they build, that construct social reality. But media play a key role in those constructions, a role that cuts so deep that its consequences are often ambiguous.

Consider two examples. In Brazil, the platform WhatsApp is hugely popular: more Brazilians use WhatsApp even than the 65% of Brazilians who have internet access, which means that multiple people are accessing WhatsApp via the same phone. What difference does this make to Brazilian society? It's complicated. Yes, Brazil is a society where truck drivers can mobilize a protest faster and more effectively than ever before by using WhatsApp, as happened in May 2018. But it's also a society where in October that same year WhatsApp became the main medium for spreading irresponsible political rumour and manipulation, including by extreme parties too small to get representation on national television.[2]

Turn to the USA. A terrible series of shootings in US schools over recent years, including the shootings at Marjory Stoneman Douglas High School in Parkland, Florida, in February 2018, have, over time, generated a major student campaign against lax gun laws and pro-gun culture. What causes those shootings? For a long time, media offered the story of lone males with grudges against particular people in their school. But when local journalist Dave Cullen investigated more closely he found little evidence for this. Shooters didn't appear to care whom they shot, yet they *did* care about the *media coverage* they achieved for themselves through the shootings. So media, Cullen concluded, through how they told the story of school shootings, were themselves making such shootings more likely to happen, without intending to do so.[3] Cullen has since campaigned for school shooters not to be named by the media.

This was echoed when, in the wake of the terrible massacre of Muslim worshippers in Christchurch mosques in March 2019, the New Zealand Prime Minister, Jacinda Ardern, said that the killer would never be named. This refusal to grant publicity stood in sharp contrast to the controversial circulation on social media platforms of the video the killer shot via his Go-Pro device.

Media, and the realities media construct, are an indispensable part of the order and disorder that make up 'our' world, the worlds of those we love or fear, 'the' world. If you have picked up this book, you probably are already disposed to believe *that* media matter. By exploring *how* media matter, I hope to convince you that you are right, and that media are worth studying closely and with all the subtlety we can muster.

In this book, I invite you to imagine a world *with* media. We will do so by exploring *five dimensions of what media do in the world*, dimensions that may not immediately occur to us when we think about media. Chapter 1 ('Connecting') considers how media technologies are able to connect up people and things, and through that connection help create something like a world. This is the first thing that human beings achieve through media. Chapter 2 ('Representing') turns to the contents that media transmit, and asks how, and with what consequences, media represent parts of our world back to us, the human beings who live in that same world. Chapter 3 ('Imagining') goes deeper into the details of the worlds media contents make, exploring the extraordinary ways in which consuming media helps us imagine our world differently, but also looking beneath the surface of digital platforms, such as Facebook, at the hidden processes of counting and categorization through data processing that make those platforms function as they do. Chapter 4 ('Sharing') moves back to our social experiences of media as users, in particular the experience of sharing things through media; for sharing is one of the basic ways in which societies hang together. Finally, Chapter 5 ('Governing') switches to the largest scale and considers governments' relations to media: do particular types of media help or hinder particular types of government?

Throughout I will be asking whether the worlds that today's media make possible are to be celebrated or feared. Perhaps the answer is 'both'.

1

Connecting

Media are technologies for transmitting and preserving what the media industry calls 'content': symbols, images, and sounds that have meaning. Meaning is a basic dimension of human life: a world which had no meaning, and made absolutely no sense to us, would be a terrifying world indeed. So media, by circulating meanings, play a role in making our lives liveable: by circulating meanings from one place to another, they connect up spaces, and help build territories. Connecting is the first way in which media help construct the worlds we live in. But how they do this is complex.

Suppose you built a way of connecting people who didn't normally meet that helped them discover things they had in common. Suppose what you built worked fine, and you then raised the resources to convert your discovery into something sustainable. Suppose more and more people started using your platform, linking their lives to the space of connection that you had built. Scale this up a few hundred-million-fold, and you start to get a sense of something that has become commonplace in the twenty-first century.

Welcome to a key paradox of how media operate in contemporary society: simply by connecting up lots of people, and allowing those people to connect to each other, media take on a form of power *in society* – a power over how society is constructed – that their developers did not necessarily intend to acquire. This paradox has affected all the media technologies of the past four centuries, yet each age faces a distinctive version of it, ours included.

Today's paradox of media power derives from the scale and speed at which media connect up people and things, and the intricacy of how those connections are woven into the fabric of our lives. Think back, once more, to the unease the media deprivation exercise causes for many who attempt it. This brings out media's implications for power and how societies operate, implications that are real: for the people platforms connect, for those who remain unconnected, and for the vast majority of people who just use the connection without influence over how it is organized.

In the contemporary era, it makes sense to think about media not just as a single medium (television, radio, a particular digital platform or app), but as linked infrastructures that make possible a certain way of living. I will call these *infrastructures of connection*. This concept will help us think of what's both distinctive *and* universal about the world that media help make today.

Media, as infrastructures of connection, have throughout history faced constraints: the need for a medium to *carry* the meaning (stone, papyrus, parchment, paper, or even the air, in the case of message by torch relay); the need for substances to *mark* the medium (from tools to cut into it, to ink or fire); and usually also the need for material means to help the medium *cross* space (copper wires, radio waves, the moving human body, horses, even pigeons).

Across history, different infrastructures of connection have involved completely different balances of constraint and opportunity. When the carrying medium was heavy, and transport was difficult, media were largely a local affair. Media then worked more to connect people through *time* than across space. Mesopotamian clay tablets, from as early as 2000 BCE, stored important cultural, political, economic, and astronomical information for later eras. The Incas in South America used complex knotted strings called *khipus* to record bureaucratic data. The *sillok* records of Korea's Joseon dynasty, initially handwritten but printed from the early fifteenth century CE, preserved an account of the king's activities for future generations which remained secret until the king's own death. This generated the longest continuous dynastic record in world history.

The predominant challenges of twenty-first-century media are almost the opposite to those faced when writing was invented. It is now so easy to send messages and texts (even of huge size and complexity) across *space* that it is reliable storage through time which becomes difficult. And then there are human beings' limits. When media transmissions are no longer scarce but overwhelming in their frequency, the issue is how people can keep up with the flood of media messages sent their way, let alone select and preserve what is important to them.

In this chapter, we look further into the history of how media have connected people and things, before considering the complexities of social connection in an age of smartphones and social media platforms. That will give us a starting point for evaluating the different ways in which media might connect us, and their implications for the quality of human life. Perhaps, just as humans began a few decades ago to think of their physical world as an environment, an ecology, that they could help manage better or worse, so now we need an environmental (even ecological) way of thinking about media.

A History of Connection: Some High Points

Media technologies have been connecting human beings for four thousand years. The story is usually told in terms of a progression towards ever more reliable, regular, and frequent media, operating on ever-increasing geographical scales, and with ever greater intensity.

A high point in that history was the invention of the printing press. There was the introduction of the mechanical printing press and moveable type in the fifteenth century by German inventor Johannes Gutenberg, but similar technologies had already been used in China and Korea for hundreds of years. In the European case, printing led to increased circulation of religious texts, including versions of the Bible written in the languages of everyday speech. In many countries, higher levels of literacy emerged alongside new types of 'high-speed' text – the pamphlet, the novel, the newspaper – designed for fast production, wide circulation, and high-speed consumption.

It is common to see in this history of printing technology the birth of the modern era itself. But if media connect *people* and transmit the meanings they want to share, then they must always involve more than technology. The changing role of written media in Western societies over the seventeenth, eighteenth, and nineteenth centuries involved not just printing, but new forms of social and economic organization: the emergence of markets for books; gatherings where people read books together; new institutions of media (newspapers, magazines, the postal system). As media connect us, new social forms build around them.

It would be foolish, however, to ignore the practical basis of media as technologies. At certain points in history, technologies of transmission changed fundamentally. Decisive moments included the invention of the telegraph in the 1830s and the laying of land and undersea cables for transmitting messages over great distances from the 1860s. In the early twentieth century, radio and television changed not just what meanings could be communicated, but their speed of transmission. Political leaders became able, through radio, to speak instantly and directly to crowds who were not physically present with them. Television added the possibility of simultaneously transmitting a visual image, enabling distant audiences to feel as if they were present with and looking at the politician speaking to them.

The most dramatic evidence that media were connecting the world in new ways came with the sinking of the *Titanic* in April 1912. Distress signals sent by radio from the boat reached surrounding ships and listening stations on the Canadian East Coast, which then sent news of the disaster to the USA and Europe, from where many of the passengers came. Within hours, there was a spreading awareness of an international disaster unfolding in a shared present. Along with a vivid new sense of the immediacy of news came a huge marketing opportunity for Enrico Marconi, whose radio technology and listening stations made the messages possible.

Media, if we understand them as infrastructures of connection, are inseparable from the history of economic power and political control. The intense interest of governments in information systems goes back at least to the French Revolution in the eighteenth century, but let's stay with the twentieth century. In the 1930s, Marconi came to work closely with the Italian Fascist leader Benito Mussolini as head of the latter's National Research Council. The rise of both Fascism and Nazism is unthinkable without their bold uses of electronic media to reach whole nations through the airwaves.

A few decades later, it was global television that enabled hundreds of millions of people to watch key moments of history; indeed the experience of large populations watching together was part of what made those events *into* history. Think of the inauguration of Nelson Mandela in 1994, the funeral of Princess Diana in 1997, the victory speech of Barack Obama in 2008. Yet 1994 was also the year when the world wide web became more widely available and a new infrastructure seeped into every life: the internet. There are many places on earth where internet connection is still non-existent or intermittent. But the world has nearly 9 billion mobile devices with built-in internet connection (tablets and smartphones).[1] Internet connection is now part of the *potential* of human life almost everywhere, even if phones without internet connection remain important for text messaging and payment systems (for example, the M-Pesa system used in much of Africa).

The internet has provided the backbone on which many other features of the contemporary world have been built, features that have become so basic that we find it hard to imagine the world without them: that is, the world wide web and social media platforms. Today we are experiencing a historic new phase of human interconnection through media with major implications for economic order and political power. We'll come back to political power, but first let's consider how media connections have affected how we can act in the world.

Connections and Actions

It used to be lonely being a fan, even if what you were a fan of (say, a TV show, a film, or a band) was widely popular. Why? Because, although it was media that gave you access to the object of your fandom, and sometimes you could meet other fans, for example at a concert, you had to endure the times in-between: the times when there was no one to talk to about what you loved.

The word 'fan' has roots in ancient religious cults,[2] but in the past two decades the phenomenon it describes has been transformed out of all recognition. Through platforms such as Instagram and Twitter, and even basic email and messaging, fans can be in touch and sharing their thoughts with each other continuously and from wherever they are. They can get the sense of being in touch directly – and constantly! – with the celebrities they follow.

They can share not just thoughts, but images, mash-ups, jokey video loops (GIFs), and other humorous, or serious, tokens, from moment to moment with like-minded fans across the world. All this depends on the space of connection we call the internet.

Switch the channel of enthusiasm to politics, and there is something similar going on. 'Fans' of a politician or party or policy – normally called supporters, members, voters – can be in touch with each other to swap ideas, jokes, proposals, and rumours. They can share their fury, despair, or joy at political events with those who they can be confident will share those feelings. Yes, politics is often more nationally focused than fandom, but there are plenty of international movements too, some disturbing (such as far-right extremism), that have been stimulated by the possibility of online connection.

On public or semi-public platforms like Facebook or Twitter, political fans may also meet those who do *not* share their feelings, and perhaps represent the polar opposite of their view of the world, some-times with explosive results. There are rivalries in many areas of fandom, but because politics is a concentrated space of competition, and because the stakes of political conflict can be life or death, enrichment or impoverishment, media have more disturbing implications for politics than for, say, music fandom. We talk of the polarization of politics, the decay of media's public sphere, threats even to democracy itself.

For good or ill, media have changed the practicalities of politics. Through today's social media platforms, it is now much easier to mobilize support for political action. No need any more to hand out leaflets on a street corner or go knocking on doors. Online groups can grow fast because their members can quickly spread the word to others. Messages, invitations, or provocations can spread even faster. As I worked on much of this book, the fast-spreading protests of the *gilets jaunes* in France were just the latest example.

Inspired by this practical change in how media work to mobilize through connections, some write of Facebook Revolutions (Egypt, 2011), hashtag movements (the Indignados, Spain, 2013), or a WhatsApp First election (Karnataka, India, May 2018).[3] But there is something profoundly misleading about these labels. Understanding *why* helps us see the complexity of what it means to connect.

Let's take the case of Egypt and its failed revolution in 2011. Here, as in other countries in the Middle East, social media platforms made a significant difference to how the general population were mobilized at speed and with precision for short-term action. But that was only the start of the difference media made. For, by connecting *every* point in space and time, media changed the starting point for every political actor in Egypt, including powerful actors such as governments and the army. In the long run – sometimes the short run too – governments have more ability to take advantage of new media tools for mobilization and influence than the individuals and groups who oppose them. New media opportunities for protesters do not make existing forms of power (military, governmental, legal, rhetorical) simply disappear. And so, in Egypt, military power stabilized and then came to dominate the situation, halting the revolution through plain old-fashioned violence. In recent years, government surveillance via Facebook and other social media has intensified.[4]

The new online political environment, which is so dependent on social media, brings considerable risks for activists. Even if their actions are organized on a platform which is supposedly free of surveillance (such as the encrypted WhatsApp), there are other dangers. People and computer programs who use the platform may not be what they seem. Misinformation can spread, and security-service traps be laid, as happened in the May 2018 Brazilian national truckers' strike mentioned in the introduction.

Connecting

The financial and marketing benefits for the corporations that operate digital platforms are today as obvious as they were for Marconi and his radio signals a century ago. More subtle, because they require more strategic planning, are the advantages that flow for governments from today's intensified forms of technological connection. Before we look specifically at governments, can we extract any principles from what we've considered so far?

First, media, as infrastructures of connection, create new spaces for interaction. Second, such spaces are potentially spaces of conflict, where each actor applies all the power she/he/it can muster. Third, media only connect us against the background of previous distributions of power (social and economic power; governmental, military, and broader political power). Fourth, this means the new balance of power between larger and smaller actors that results from everyone being more connected through media is profoundly uncertain.

Orders of Connection

Such shifting balances of power are crucial to understanding how media have provided resources to institutions whose goal is to impose order: that

23

is, governments. Throughout history, governments and states have been interested in media and communications. Examples are the Persian Empire, with its extensive network of horse-mounted couriers, and the Roman Empire, whose scale meant that emperors needed to 'govern by correspondence'.[5] Some historians argue that the decisive moment in the emergence of the modern state in twelfth-century Europe was the increasing use by rulers of writing (on parchment) to record decisions and to track their implementation.[6]

The interests of government in media's infrastructures of connection are sometimes forgotten as we celebrate those who use media from the margins. The steady rise to global power of the People's Republic of China, however, shows why optimistic stories about how more media 'must free us' are deeply misleading. Although its starting points for developing internet connection were very different from those in the West, China has over the past decade developed social media platforms that are directly comparable. These are, nevertheless, organized in a distinctive way: very large Chinese platforms (think Alibaba for Amazon, TenCent for Facebook, Baidu for Google) have closer links to government and much deeper functional integration. Imagine combining Facebook with Amazon *and then* adding in financial platforms, all with considerable state encouragement and support, and you come close to the power of the Chinese *super-platforms* today. It is the system of super-platforms which makes possible the Chinese government's plans to introduce a 'social credit system' for managing the Chinese population by tracking their behaviour online and rating them accordingly (more on this in Chapter 5).

The Chinese government does not hide its policy goals. It has proclaimed a vision of *a fully connected society* where economy, citizens, and state work in harmony through infrastructures of connection and the continuous monitoring and processing of data. To get a flavour of this vision, here's a quote from China's Internet Plus policy published in 2014:

> [F]ully give rein to the superiority of scale and application of our country's internet . . . accelerate the enhancement of industrial development levels, strengthen innovation capabilities in all sectors, build new economic and social development superiorities and functions. Persist in reform, innovation, and orientation towards market demand . . . and forcefully expand the breadth and depth of the internet's convergence with all areas of the economy and society.

This vision of media's connective role in society, though its language about innovation overlaps with how Western governments see the development of the internet, has very different implications for freedom. Its main emphasis is on social order, not individual freedom.

To sum up, media create not only new tools with which citizens can speak up and resist, but also new tools with which governments can manage and govern society. This is a theme to which we shall return in the final chapter. If you are concerned about such visions of control, it is not only governments that you should fear. Remember it was Google's former CEO, Eric Schmidt, who said that 'if you have something that you don't want anyone to know, maybe you shouldn't be doing it in the first place'.[7] Google for sure know what we want to search for: their business model is based on that knowledge.

Understanding how media of many types connect societies is key to grasping what sorts of government are likely to rule us in the twenty-first century, democratic or otherwise.

A Connected Life?

Media connections also have profound implications for our interactions with those close to us. Once again, the results are ambiguous: media give us extra ways of acting in the world, but bring new constraints and obligations. Media ensure not only that we connect, but that we *are connected*.

For some people, the pressures of a life connected through media are so intense that every so often they need to detox. But the advantages that flow daily from how media connect us are impossible to dispute. For one thing, media enable us to access more easily the information we need to travel between places. That's why the mobile phone has become an indispensable tool for the millions of forced migrants on the move, at high risk, in desperate search for better conditions of life.

Smartphone interfaces have taken on a vital role in many families. In many instances, job opportunities are so scarce that family members choose to migrate to find adequately paid employment, for example the large migrant worker populations in the Middle East or Europe. Often, those workers maintain parenting relations with children back home, in the Philippines and elsewhere. More privileged families can also benefit from keeping in touch with each other and with friends more continuously than ever before as they move around for pleasure or work.

Does this mean that, overall, human beings are now connected through media to a wider range of people than in previous periods? This is what marketers often claim. But the evidence, from the introduction of the telephone onwards, is that people tend to use new media technologies to connect most to those they already know: that is, family and friends.[8] The more important question therefore is not to whom media connect us, but whether or not intensified connection with those to whom we are already connected improves our intimate lives.

Within families, there is a very complex play of forces to consider. The great Russian novelist Tolstoy once wrote that 'all happy families are alike' – happy in the same way – but 'an unhappy family is unhappy after its own fashion'.[9] We know for sure that happy families are using media to keep in touch regularly, to find new ways of being spontaneous together, to archive their memories more effectively, to coordinate better what they do. But this is not the whole story.

Some disturbing patterns are already apparent. First, there are the growing fears that media provide too easy an escape route from the tedium or oppression of family life, generating forms of screen-time addiction, particularly for young people, that the World Health Organization includes within its definition of 'substance abuse'.[10] Second, media can be brought *into* family interactions in disturbing ways. Media recording devices are today present in spaces that previously would have been free of them, such as a couple's bedroom. This is fine while the relationship is going well, but when things go wrong, the ugly practice of 'revenge porn' can ensue. Increasingly recognized as a crime in many countries, this act is almost always committed by men against women.

The smartphone's capacity to circulate images instantly and on a large scale has been dubbed by one sociologist 'mass self-communication':[11] DIY broadcasting, if you like. But sometimes it is not the 'self' that is broadcast. Emerging alongside the smartphone, and less noticed, has been the spy-cam. Media can be a tool for broadcasting the intimacy *of others* when it is absolutely *not* wanted. Consider 'upskirting', which various countries are considering making a criminal offence, and '*molka*', secretly filmed images of a sexual nature, which has generated a rising tide of arrests in South Korea.[12] Once again, these acts are generally perpetrated by men against women.

These disturbing features are an important part of the emerging order – or should we say, *disorder*? – of media societies. They are just as much part of what it means for people to live in a 'connected' world as is the happy swapping of pictures of food, family get-togethers, or smiling friends.

Conclusion: Media as Ecology

This brings into focus an issue that has run through-out the chapter. Media, by connecting us more and in new ways, do not have simple implications for power relations; rather they provide new tools for power, new spaces for conflict and, hopefully, cooperation too. It is misguided, although common, to expect from media outcomes that are universally 'good' or universally 'bad'. How could such neat outcomes flow when media connect up billions of people and enable them to do almost *whatever* they want to do?

Media connect up our worlds in complex ways. We appreciate this when we consider the web of interrelations that we live through media. There are so many interrelated things that we do through media, and that media do to us, that it makes sense to think of all this as an *environment*, an environment *for living* today. We have no problem thinking about the spaces where other animals live together as environments. Indeed, in biology or zoology, we would never talk about single animals, or even single food sources, but about whole *ecologies* of interacting elements – ecologies that, as we are all now sadly aware, can be woefully out of balance.

Thinking *ecologically* about media means considering not just what media technologies we use, but also what the consequences are of media over the longer term for how we interrelate to each other as human beings. A key feature of the contemporary media ecology, which makes it very different from earlier phases in media history, is that it is *interactive*. Provided a computer is at hand, we can each send *and* receive a message from any point in space. With the internet, and its so-called 'end-to-end' architecture, any of us, in principle, can now 'broadcast' a message to as many destinations as we want; we can also rely on others to pass on that message. This means that our uses of the internet – the choices we make about what images to send, what images to open – are not separate from, but part of, media's ecology.

Yet media, in connecting us, build on the power dynamics that were *already* shaping people's relations to each other in workplaces and schools, families and friendship networks, religious movements and political associations, and between classes, genders, generations, and races. Through the connections they make possible, media help shape the present, but always on the foundations of the past. And as they shape particular societies, media also represent societies back to their members in some form, whether they recognize themselves in media's mirror or not. In the next chapter, we turn to how those processes of representation work, and the benefits and risks they generate.

2

Representing

What usually draws our attention to media are not connections, but representations. We are excited by the reality that media present to us here and now: the excitement of a game on live TV, the look of a new fashion model who is turning heads. We feel media's power in the anger that a news image provokes in us, or the desire we feel to be part of the world that a film portrays.

Representing is the other side of connecting. Yes, media are infrastructures of connection, but media are also the meanings that circulate *through* those infrastructures of connection, meanings that present the world back to us. Like all representations, they can be rich, ambiguous, and open to conflicting interpretation. It follows that media are both infrastructure *and* meaning, or medium *and* message (to recall the language of 1960s Canadian media theorist Marshall McLuhan).

How then do media represent the world? That is the question strategic communicators in politics and marketing must master. It's not enough just to reach people, to have a basic connection; you need to figure out what to do with that connection, how to use it to get someone to act as you want. Representing is usually about persuading too.

Media present us with worlds that we might never otherwise see: the animals hidden in a distant jungle or at the bottom of the ocean; a political or celebrity scandal that it took months for media to uncover; a signing ceremony to which only press and senior politicians were invited; a catwalk planned only for fashion industry insiders. When media present us with these distant worlds, it is tempting to believe that through media we literally *access* the worlds that we see, but that is to forget the role that media organizations and their employees play in selecting what story they present to us.

Sometimes, to bring us back to the reality of what media do, it is worth writing the word 'representing' with a hyphen, as in '*re*-presents'. Media present us with a world for our reactions, involvement, and disgust, but this is always a *re*-presentation, just *one*

34

way that media have chosen to present to us what they have heard, read, and seen. Whole libraries of research on the workings of media organizations lie behind that simple statement. In this chapter, we will stay at a fairly abstract level, in order to bring out some general features of how media represent the world. But remember throughout that behind the processes we discuss are always specific journalists and other media workers, using their skills and exercising choices under particular working conditions (choices over editing, programme scheduling, and relations to advertisers; judgements about news values and the ethics of showing this or that image).

Re-presentation: that hyphen gets us straight to some of the most complex issues to which media give rise. This chapter starts by introducing the basic puzzle of how media's representations make a difference in the world: the puzzle of media 'effects'. From there we'll consider the role that media representations play in politics, particularly democratic politics. In the chapter's last part, we'll think more about the conflicts over representation in which media become involved and the unexpected demands placed on social media platforms that, it seems, only wanted to connect us, not to represent the world at all.

Representing

Thinking about Media 'Effects'

Let's take a media image at random: say, Beyoncé performing at the 2016 Super Bowl Halftime Show. We know that the producers of the image – especially those close to Beyoncé – would have liked it to have impact, to persuade those who encountered it of something important. But how? How, seriously, are we to think about the difference that one image makes as it is reproduced on millions of newspaper covers, circulated on gossip and other websites and through people's social media posts, talked about in countless public and private settings, mimicked by people at work or in bars, recycled in countless later news and comment articles?

Asking the barely answerable question of media 'effects' leads us into the labyrinth of how media meanings make a difference in the complex world that media connect. If media matter, they must have *some* consequences (there must be *some* way of emerging from the labyrinth with a story to tell). But establishing those consequences is surprisingly difficult. How much do we know about the varied responses to a performance like Beyoncé's and the long-term implications of such a performance as they resonate through wider society? For some, Beyoncé might be a role model, for others, not.

To grasp how media's representations work in society, we must go back nearly half a century to the early writings of one of the world's most famous theorists of race and identity: the late Stuart Hall.

In September 1973, Hall gave a presentation to a Council of Europe conference called 'Training in the Critical Reading of Television'. Hall pointed out the crudeness of most attempts to interpret how television makes a difference in society. He mocked psychological approaches that interpreted media 'effects' like a stimulus-response in a laboratory. What was needed, Hall argued, was to understand how an actual viewer *interprets* a programme from *their* world, and how that interpretation intersects, or not, with the interpretation that the producers of the programme had intended.[1]

The model Hall developed had enormous influence in media research. I want to focus not on the detail, but on the simple, if radical, move that Hall had made. By insisting that what people make of programmes cannot be determined in advance by the programme makers themselves, Hall opened up a neglected issue in the social sciences: how do *actual* audiences make sense of the vast numbers of images and texts that circulate in their culture? What Hall put his finger on was not just the complexity of how meanings are built into media production (the media 'text'), but the complexity of what audiences actually do with that text. This, as it happens, was the question which drew me into thinking about media twenty-five years ago: the area of research called 'audience studies'.

The world of media flows online is today massively more complex than the one Hall considered back in a 1970s Britain of three TV channels. Yet Hall already realized that real people interpret media from a range of different positions. Those positions are not random but shaped by their experience of life and by their position in society (their class, gender, race, sexuality). Workers and managers are unlikely to interpret news coverage of a strike in which they are involved the same way; they probably interpret business news differently too. This insight is important for understanding a diverse and highly conflicted society such as the USA with its politically polarized media.

Another key point that emerged in 1990s research, but which is even more important in the age of social media, was that the contexts and situations in which media meanings reach people can be hugely varied. Some contexts are conducive to sitting down and carefully working out the meaning of a programme, but they are relatively rare. More often, media give us a glancing blow, like a post we scroll through on our phone. We *may* focus on that text for a short period, but our memory of it is quickly overwhelmed by the many other texts which crowd in upon us.

Much of what we, as audiences, do with media can be understood as what in the 1930s the great German cultural theorist Walter Benjamin called 'reception in a state of distraction'. American novelist Don DeLillo revived this theme for the late twentieth-century world of multiple cable TV channels. In *White Noise*, DeLillo reflected on a culture overflowing with media messages; '[t]he world', he writes, 'is full of abandoned meanings'.[2]

And yet some images do matter. Advertisers and marketers invest all their energies in trying to draw us out of our distraction and towards more engaged interpretation. But the media environment in which advertisers try to get our attention has become ever more complex, as the media environment has become more dense *and* more varied in the digital era. Thirty years ago, an audience researcher could assume that people got their news by following a national live news bulletin broadcast at fixed times of the day, or by reading a newspaper printed the night before. In the twenty-first century, such simplicities have disappeared, even though news bulletins and newspapers continue. Who, a decade ago, would have expected that by 2018 YouTube (a video website owned by Google) would be the main form in which almost half of UK 12- to 15-year-olds watch television?[3] Many people of all ages in many countries now get their main news from the 'feeds' of social media platforms.

In areas such as fashion or politics, marketers are investing considerable resources in trying to influence this process. The question of who influences our interpretations of news was already a key theme of 1950s media research. But 'influencers' – a fashionable term today – represent just one attempt to order a much more complex process.

Another key factor is attention. You may have heard the phrase 'economy of attention'. This is a core issue in marketing today, because it is hard – extremely hard – to get anyone to pay attention to a specific message in a world where too many people and entities (think of bots) are trying to speak all at once. We have never known exactly how different people's attention to news varies, but we can be sure it varies a lot because of prior knowledge or interest, and the factors which might shape this (class, gender, occupation).

To sum up: if media representations have effects, these are necessarily complex. *That* media representations make a difference somehow is, however, beyond doubt, and it is the nagging insistence that they do which underlies many scare stories about media over recent decades. It is time to consider those larger questions and their implications for society, politics, and democracy.

Media Representations and the Possibility of Democratic Politics

Media represent the world in particular ways, by making detailed selections and choices about how to present what they see as important. How they do this has consequences for politics. For democracies cannot function at all without media representations. Two and a half centuries ago, some fondly imagined that a modern democracy could be built on the decisions of people who actually met together face-to-face, as citizens did in ancient Athens. This at least was Jean-Jacques Rousseau's eighteenth-century vision in his essay *The Social Contract*. But we absolutely cannot imagine this today. 'The people' that speaks through contemporary democracies' political processes is a people represented in and through media. Media institutions do not stand in for people literally, as politicians do, but they present the 'reality' of what the people are thinking or feeling: this reality becomes the reference point for political debate and decision-making.

There are two fundamentally different ways in which media, by representing the life around them, can support democracy: first, they can encourage political affinities; second, they can present an adequate picture of the changing world as a reference point for democratic decision-making. The two are closely related, but let's take them separately. The first involves media identifying the *demos* (Greek for 'people') that is democracy's *subject*. The second involves media identifying the reality over which the people's power is to be exercised: that is, the *object* of democratic politics.

Another eighteenth-century political theorist, Edmund Burke, had an important insight into the roots of political engagement. Those roots lie, he argued, not in fully formed political allegiances but in something deeper: our care for family and friends, what Burke called 'the little platoon we belong to in society'. But what does this mean today? If Burke was right, politics in large and complex societies where most people never meet with each other can only be based on millions of people somehow sharing a bond, some new basis of emotional connection. That bond today is enabled, in large part, through media.

Media provide the materials out of which we can imagine some closeness to people whom we are never likely to meet. The result is what historian Benedict Anderson called 'imagined communities'. For Anderson, media such as the newspaper and novel from the mid-eighteenth century onwards played a key role in populations both in the West and beyond imagining themselves as nations. As such, media were much more than economic ventures; they were ways in which in expanding societies people began living *together* in the same time and the same territory. Without common media, it is hard to see how democratic politics, indeed any politics, would be possible in large societies.

Media construct a sense of what is shared and normal, what is 'just there' to be lived through in common. But here we confront the crux of what is difficult to grasp about media's representational role in contemporary societies. In our private lives, there *is* no simple reality. There is always a choice of which story you listen to and, before that, a choice as to whom you listen to. But if the same uncertainty applied in the spaces where millions of people struggle to live their lives in parallel (a nation), there would be chaos. One institution for avoiding such chaos is 'media': the work done by small numbers of institutions to present to a territory a common reality that, over time, most citizens come to treat as beyond dispute.

Sometimes media's work in stabilizing 'reality' is successful, sometimes not. Think of media's stories about 'the weather': generally, we don't dispute their veracity. More contentious are the stories about the major issues that a territory must resolve politically at a particular time. As I write, Brexit is one such issue in the UK; the status of the US/ Mexican border is another in the USA.

A key question for the quality of politics in a particular territory is who can influence media's stories of 'what is going on' in that territory (and who cannot). Here it is difficult to keep apart what we just imagined were two separate levels: media's role in representing the subject of democratic politics, and media's role in representing the object of democratic politics.

Consider migration. Are the living conditions that drive migrants to try to enter mainland Europe or cross the southern US border one of the realities that European and US media should cover as a basic matter for citizens to think about? Your answer will differ depending on whether you see those migrants as people with whom the European and US populations should have some affinity, or as clear outsiders. Media construct both sides of that story: they help construct the affinities that orient audiences *towards* people 'close' to them, and *away* from those to whom they are, supposedly, not close.

At the very heart of the modern nation, then, are key choices, deeply political and so rarely made explicit, about what sort of human being is a member of that nation, and what sort of human being is not. History, much of it long pre-dating modern media, is hugely important here, shaping, for example, how 'First Nation' peoples are regarded in countries such as Australia, Brazil, Canada, Chile, and the USA, and how regions are presented in the UK. Contemporary media play their part in reinforcing stories of the 'natural' basis of every modern nation.

How in practice, then, do media re-present the nation and its constituent parts to itself? One basic way is through the languages in which media speak: the language of news bulletins, weather forecasts, and documentary voiceovers. Many nations have multiple languages: think of India and China; but think also of the UK, although for decades its national government and media tried to deny that languages other than English (Welsh, Gaelic) were spoken there. In the USA, meanwhile, Spanish is the first language of many millions, but not of America's dominant mainstream media.

Another way that media represent the nation to itself is through the types of people they commonly represent, whether elites (politicians, professionals, the rich and famous) or the nation's 'ordinary people'. Another is through the selections media make of news items, and the geographical bias to that selection. Still another is through the priorities media signal between different types of news story and different types of voice. A recent study of how migrants were presented by media during the European migrant 'crisis' revealed that migrants, though regularly portrayed, were rarely presented on their own terms by national media. Similar questions can be raised at the global scale: who chooses which countries regularly lead global news bulletins and how their actions are portrayed? Those questions are especially important for areas of intense political conflict, for example the Middle East and Latin America.

There are interesting implications here for geopolitics. Which nation's media have most chance of influencing the agendas of global news at any one time? For a long period, the international influence of US media on news agendas has been strong, but this may be changing. Even at the national level the very possibility of democracy is affected by how good or bad a job media institutions do in representing the struggles for resources and recognition that we call 'politics'.

Battles for Voice, Battles for the Image

Perhaps we can go further and suggest that media representations shape the boundaries of politics itself. If so, it matters hugely who is doing the shaping. There are many parties to these conflicts: powerful employees of media institutions, such as news editors, documentary directors, and screenplay writers; political or social organizations that challenge media stories or try to influence them; and the journalists whose by-line may be on the story that gets published.

Much of the history of media can be told in terms of battles over representation. Particular genres, such as the soap opera or in Latin America the *telenovela*, have become important as places where battles of representation can be fought: battles over the representation of sexuality, drugs, violence, or racial prejudice. Representation battles arise also in relation to ways or styles of speaking. From the 1980s, talk shows became important spaces for sharing issues informally, for example the lives of sexual minorities or men's domestic violence

against women, issues that had not been acknowl-
edged in media before. By the second half of the
twentieth century, British media had become less
restrictive in how non-elite voices were represented
and how everyday talk, language, and gesture were
portrayed. But all that does not mean that other
voices were not lost. In the same period, trade union
perspectives on politics and the economy became
less prominent owing to the changing advertising
base of British newspapers.

Representational successes can always be ambiguous in their consequences. The emergence of 'reality
media' formats in many countries from the early
1990s seemed a huge step forward in making 'ordinary' lives visible for national television viewing:
popular formats had versions on many continents,
and some reality formats continue to this day. But
how did this work in practice? Many shows brought
conflict between classes and genders into this new
forum, subtly or unsubtly reinforcing pre-existing
prejudices, for example by showing working-class
couples how (from a middle-class perspective) they
'should' decorate their home. You can almost hear
the judgemental tone in the titles of some UK series:
What Not To Wear, How Clean is Your House?

One positive development in the past decade has
been the expansion across social media of forums

for such battles over representation to be played out. Digital platforms have become sites for intense conflict over how daily or political life gets represented. Conflicts over racial politics in the USA long pre-date contemporary media. But platforms such as Twitter have provided important spaces for organizations to contest representational issues. Although the Black Lives Matter movement in the USA did not begin as a hashtag, its swift rise to national attention in 2014 owed much to the fluidity of Twitter as a medium. So too with the MeToo movement, which has challenged male sexual exploitation of women, first in the film industry, but then much more broadly.

Against these positive examples, however, must be weighed the everyday pressure through media of the dominant moral consensus that makes challenging power so difficult. There is plenty of uncivil abuse online, for example against migrants, that it is intimidating to challenge.[4] Here, as in other domains, new patterns of representation mask practices – regulatory, economic, labour – which reinforce existing power structures.

Representing

Media's Missing Conscience?

The landscapes of media have varied hugely between different eras. Some have been dominated by large media channels; others have offered a more varied landscape of small and large media outlets. The decades before the French Revolution of 1789 were characterized by a proliferation of small-scale media, such as the pamphlet, that operated to challenge the large narratives of society and politics on which existing power relied. These small media made an important contribution to the decline in the French monarchy's legitimacy. A very different story might be told of revolutions in Eastern Europe in 1989 when mainstream media, particularly cross-border satellite television, proved an extremely important forum for presenting the collapse of the Communist regimes.

Much of the twentieth century can be understood in terms of the rise to power of large-scale media corporations, often with huge national reach and legitimacy, such as the BBC in the UK and Doordarshan in India. These large-scale media broadcast some of those nations' most important moments, whether events such as the coronation of Elizabeth II in 1953 or Winston Churchill's funeral in 1965 in the UK or national dramas such as India's *Ramayana* TV series in 1986–8.

Representing

The world of the emerging internet was promoted by some as offering 'the daily me', a democratized form of media production by contrast with the mass media era.⁵ Has the twenty-first-century media's apparently more decentred landscape changed fundamentally how media represent complex social realities? It is hard to tell. In many countries, two contradictory forces are unfolding.

On the one hand, everyday media users today have a clear alternative to official news sources' representations of their reality: that alternative is social media. Many, for example, in the USA, UK, or Brazil now treat social media as their main news source, not official broadcast bulletins or newspapers. It is not that demand for something like news has disappeared. News of *some* sort remains the site where a society's struggle to frame its contentious issues still goes on. But the category of 'news' has become unstable. News on social media platforms means whatever those platforms present to people in, say, their Facebook newsfeed, regardless of whether the underlying source is news institutions, friends' comments, or, notoriously, lies propagated by bots or the automated recommendations of search engines such as Google or, in South Korea, Naver. Both Facebook and Naver were plagued by scandal in 2017 and 2018 because of evidence of hidden manipulation; issues of unwitting racial bias in Google search results also became controversial.

Such scandals had their roots in the problem, mentioned in the last chapter, that a more interconnected world poses for advertisers: how to reach those they need to reach with their messages? In response, advertisers began reprioritizing where they spent their advertising money, diverting money away from ads in traditional journalism outlets to simply tracking consumers wherever they are online. The long-term effect has been to change profoundly the economic stability of journalism and newspapers, in particular. Meanwhile, people start to give more credence to whatever their friends circulate on social media, including sources from which media make no income. Here deep economic and social forces, working within and around media institutions, are changing what can be represented as part of our daily 'reality'.

On the other hand, democracies' need for reliable sources of news continues. Some argue this need is growing, because today's intensified web of media connection lures many of us into 'media bubbles', where broadcast news becomes a faint flicker on the wall of our prejudices. Meanwhile, new institutions are being asked to take responsibility for how social reality is represented – entities bizarrely ill suited to the task. Take Facebook. Even a cursory knowledge of its business history shows that it never intended to become an arbiter of news value. Its goal was always the profits that could be made by connecting people, increasingly from the advertising opportunities this generated. For a long time, Facebook even denied that it was a news publisher, claiming the status of a neutral intermediary. But, given the planetary scale of its so-called 'community' and its role as a source of 'what's going on', Facebook has faced inexorable pressure to take responsibility for what gets circulated through its platforms.

How did Facebook get into the position of presenting to us something like news? Not by employing journalists! Instead it used algorithms, techniques of automated calculation that sort out the countless traffic on social media sites into the edited format that we see, for example, on our newsfeeds. We will look more into how algorithms work in the next chapter, but for now the key point is that the way algorithms work is itself driven by deep business choices about what benefits Facebook. Algorithms were never intended to generate reliable journalistic representations of the social world. Yet such is democracies', and societies', need for *some* institution which takes responsibility for the information that circulates in their territory that Facebook has been pushed into attempting to meet such expectations. But its algorithms cannot possibly replicate the decades-long skill of an experienced journalist.[6]

Facebook's limits were exposed in March 2018 by a major scandal. This involved the now defunct lobbying and psychological influence company Cambridge Analytica, a heavy user of Facebook data. Cambridge Analytica used data extracted from Facebook to target messages at the platform's users designed to influence their political actions, having used that data to calculate those users' propensities to vote in particular ways. People were shocked that the world represented to them through their newsfeeds might have become a medium for personally targeted propaganda. The questions raised by this scandal over social media platforms' role in democracy are still unresolved.

Conclusion: Evaluating Media's Symbolic Power

In this chapter, we have applied an environmental, even ecological, way of thinking about media to one of the most complex things that media do: represent what is happening in the world back to its inhabitants. By sustaining our attention to their representations, media do more than just represent specific things. They acquire a distinctive sort of power, the power that French sociologist Pierre Bourdieu once called 'a power of constructing reality'.[7] This power is based on concentrations of economic power: it requires huge economic resource to launch a television station or a large-scale social media platform. But the direct resources that media use to exercise this power are not economic, but symbolic: symbols, images, texts, and increasingly, in the age of digital media, software.

The question we must ask is whether, on the whole, media, including social media platforms, exercise that symbolic power for good or ill. In the past five years, this has become more than a rhetorical question. In the next chapter, we look at one of the most subtle ways that media can use their symbolic power: to shape our imaginations of the world in which we live.

3

Imagining

Media do more than connect us and represent the world. Media industries also put vast energy into producing elaborate new versions of the world in the form of television series, films, songs, and games. Through those media productions we can imagine the world differently: we gain new understandings of what the world means, and how it works. Few doubt that without media the social world would be imaginatively poorer.

I am drawing a line here between imagination and representation, since fictional media are freer in how they can present the world to us than news and documentary. But the line may not be so sharp in practice, since the main point of imagining new worlds through media fictions is usually to help us understand the actual world, but in a different light from how we normally see it.

Imagining

In this chapter, we will start by considering a range of imaginative fictions produced by the media industries, looking for continuities with earlier forms of media, such as the novel. In the chapter's second half, we turn to a very different way of imagining the social world through media, one not generally considered to be imagination. I mean the ways in which the social world is now being put together through the operation of algorithms: for example, the algorithms which perform the myriad calculations that lead to the selection of this or that particular message to appear at the top of our Facebook newsfeed.

More on algorithms later, but be warned: this chapter will move us towards a disturbing question. Could it be that our participation in today's media – today's infrastructures of connection – enables large forces, such as corporations and governments, to re-imagine the social world in *their* interest? But for now, enjoy the panorama of the imaginative visions that media have offered us over the past two centuries or more.

Imagining

Media Fictions and Social Complexity

Our story starts long before the era that most people associate with electronic media (radio, film, and television). Already in the late eighteenth century, societies that were undergoing rapid urbanization, early industrial capitalism, and the emergence of market economies needed ways of capturing the sheer complexity of what was happening. This role was played by novels. Novels are media too, mass-produced outputs of the printing press, even if their creators are single writers, not the large production teams that later became normal in newspapers and electronic media.

Consider this passage from Honoré de Balzac's great novel *Old Goriot*, published in 1834–5:

> Paris is an ocean. Throw in the plummet, you will never reach bottom. Survey it, describe it. However conscientious your survey ... however numerous and concerned to learn the truth the explorers of this sea may be, there will always be ... an unknown cavern, flowers, pearls, monsters, things undreamed of, overlooked.

The point of Balzac's novel was to unfold not just the growing complexity of French society, but also the problems that flowed from this: above all, people's failure to understand each other, or even to be curious about each other, and, as a result, their ability to be extremely cruel without even knowing it. Balzac challenges his readers on this point:

> The chariot of civilization . . . is scarcely halted by a heart less easily crushed than the others in its path . . . and you will show the same insensibility, as you hold this book in your white hand, lying back in a softly cushioned armchair, and saying to yourself, 'Perhaps this one is amusing.' But you may be certain that this drama is neither fiction nor romance.[1]

Balzac offers a vision of how media (the mass-readership novel) can enhance social understanding in societies that seem too large to comprehend. This goes beyond the idea of an imagined community, which we touched on in Chapter 2: the point, for Balzac, was to help people make sense of a world where there seemed to be *no* community. He saw the novel as a way to penetrate the non-transparency or opacity of complex societies.

Balzac was not unique among nineteenth-century European novelists in this ambition. Zola in France, Dickens in England, and Tolstoy in Russia each wanted to write novels on a scale that could capture the expanding diversity of the social worlds around them. And much of the subsequent history of film and television drama can be understood from the perspective of Balzac's great vision.

First, there is the tradition of the crime drama, which itself began with novels. From the late nineteenth century onwards, crime novels viewed the world through the eyes of a detective, for a long time male, with an extraordinary ability to see meaning in the city's apparent chaos and solve crimes that no one else could. While our image of the crime novel is often seen through the eyes of a middle-class figure like Sherlock Holmes or Hercule Poirot, however, just as important are the working-class detectives of US crime fiction, which was enormously popular among working-class audiences in the USA and Britain in the 1930s and 1940s.

The crime novel fed into the growth of crime drama in film and television from the mid-twentieth century onwards. This has taken many cultural forms. Take the Scandinavian TV crime dramas of the past decade or so, such as *The Killing* and *The Bridge*. These crime series depict the many complex forces at work in a large society: in the Danish drama *The Killing* we see the connections between police under pressure to solve a high-profile murder case; politicians and their personal secrets; the barely suppressed racism of much of the population; and the long-term consequences of socially reintegrating those who fought in distant wars. These dramas have worked very well in translation outside Scandinavia, perhaps because they offer ways of imagining the forces transforming many contemporary societies, and not just one in particular.

A very different, but equally interesting, story about media and social complexity could be told through the genre of science fiction. Again, the beginnings were in the novel. The challenge of visually presenting outer space and future worlds was particularly well suited to television and film. Digital techniques of CGI (computer-generated imagery) have vastly expanded film's capacity to show complex action and visual effects, though not necessarily to enhance film's imaginative power. Classic science fiction films such as *2001: A Space Odyssey* (1968) and *The Matrix* (1999), by presenting to us a distant future, could explore issues around the human body and mind, and our relations to the universe and the artificial intelligence that society will generate. More rarely, science fiction films bridge distant worlds and life back on earth, as in Russian director Andrei Tarkovsky's great film *Solaris* (1972), where the journey to outer space gains impact from the depiction of a tense, oppressive society on earth that precedes it.

Imagining

In the twentieth and twenty-first centuries, the speed of technological change and the capacity to experiment with the building blocks of human life have let loose within society forces which cannot, in any simple way, be seen at work in daily life, and yet which need our attention as citizens and as human beings. Are we comfortable, for example, with the unfolding power of artificial intelligence or gene editing? Film offers an important medium for focusing societal debate about such issues: *The Matrix*, for example, continues to be a reference point in public discussion on artificial intelligence.

A third example of how media help us imagine the world differently comes from the recent renaissance of large-scale drama in the world of television beyond free-to-air channels (from HBO's subscription model to pay-TV channel AMC to Netflix). Think of the shows *The Sopranos*, *The Wire*, and *Breaking Bad*.

The Wire had five series, each covering drug crime in the run-down US city of Baltimore from the perspective of a separate institution (police, trade unions, politics, education, and the media). In its huge scope, it perhaps comes closest to the ambitions of Balzac and Zola: the idea of unfolding, drama by drama, the interlocking complexity of a large society. *The Sopranos* and *Breaking Bad* continue themes from traditional crime drama, but look at crime as much from the perspective of the normal lives of those deeply embedded in it as from that of the criminal world itself. They build here on the tradition of Mafia films where 'the family' is both a crime network and a real family.

All three TV shows provide fascinating insights into the compartmentalization of moral thinking that characterizes life in complex societies. People take actions whose effects operate at a distance, allowing them, like Tony Soprano, the Mafia boss anti-hero of *The Sopranos*, to know exactly what they are doing but somehow tell themselves a very different story about what they are doing means.

We are back here to the theme of social opacity that Balzac captured at the start of *Old Goriot*. But just as important as the themes that contemporary media fictions *have* covered are the economic and social realities they have *not* covered. There has to date, for example, been no Dickens of the global poverty and environmental disasters of the late twentieth and early twenty-first centuries, and few feature films have reflected on the experiences and causes of migration.[2]

Comparable issues about representativeness arise when we turn to the imaginative fiction of media celebrity. Celebrity has always been part of the commercial package that the cinema industry has used to sell films to audiences. From early on, however, it became clear that, through the constructed 'personality' of the actor-star, something more interesting and imaginative was at work. The great Welsh media and cultural theorist Raymond Williams once said that television dramas fulfil citizens' 'need for images, for representations, of what living is now like'.[3] Today we can see celebrities doing the same, not just through their media roles, but through the details of their actual lives.

To make your life an exemplar of how others might live surely creates intense pressures for the person behind the celebrity mask. It is no longer just professional actors who face these tensions. Over the past two decades, proliferating media channels and changing economies of television production have created ever more 'ordinary' celebrities: people plucked from everyday life for temporary celebrity in reality TV shows, such as *Love Island* and *Castaway*. As the phenomenon of 'celebrity culture' has grown, particularly in the USA and UK, it has become ever less clear whether the lives that celebrities show us in exemplary form are typical of life as most people live it. Sometimes they are, and in insightful ways, but very often what we see reflects more the distortions that the privileges of celebrity themselves bring.

I could go on to describe other forms of media imagination, for example music. Music does not just provide joy and tools for self-expression and identification, but also can, like film, address larger societies' needs to face their complexities. To take one example from 2018, think of the viral success of rap artist Childish Gambino's video *This is America*.

Instead, however, I want to stretch a little our understanding of the term 'media', and consider a form of imagination that goes on in the background of media products, in ways that are largely hidden from media users. I mean the power of algorithms.

Society and the Algorithmic Imaginary

The word 'algorithm' has a beautiful history, deriving from the name of the ninth-century CE Arab mathematician Muhammad ibn Musa al-Khwarizmi. In the world of large-scale computing, algorithm refers to any automated mechanism for counting, performing calculations, and processing data repetitively. Almost all our interfaces with media today depend on algorithms in this sense, from ticketing sites to social media platforms. It might seem surprising to claim that these seemingly humble processes actually serve to *reimagine* our society. Yet Norwegian scholar Taina Bucher has gone so far as to say we live in the age of the 'algorithmic imaginary'. As we shall see, this is a plausible reading of the power of algorithms in contemporary societies.

Much of our relaxation and social time is spent on digital platforms: social media like WhatsApp and wechat, game platforms, and so on. Much of our work time is taken up interfacing with platforms that, one way or the other, monitor what we are doing. An ever-higher percentage of our consumer transactions happen online using credit cards and other forms of electronic payment. In each case, our online activities are tracked and monitored.

All these forms of monitoring involve computers. Computers cannot monitor anything without counting and processing units of information. Algorithms are automated procedures, driven by computer software, for counting and aggregating data. When we go online via a computing device, data is gathered about what we do on that device; in the process, many items get counted and compared with pre-set expectations. The resulting 'data' may help our devices function, but it also has potential economic value, since it is usable by the sites we visit, and sellable to others, especially when combined with other data gathered about us. This data processing is now basic to how media operate, and, many argue, to the operations of contemporary capitalism.

But what, you might ask, has automated data processing got to do with media's role in *imagining* society? The answer is that such tracking and processing are becoming the means to new understandings of the social world. Those understandings are not necessarily richer than those of traditional media industries, but they are certainly more useful to various commercial and governmental interests. The outputs of those understandings – in the form of predictions about how we will behave and how best we can be marketed to – are increasingly embedded in everyday life, reimagining our lives and our likely choices. How is this happening?

Services like Facebook are just the most familiar and dramatic example of a much larger trend towards reorganizing social life through software-run 'platforms'. Platforms are of two basic sorts: platforms where we go to do very specific sorts of things, such as sell or buy something on eBay; and platforms where we go to hang out and pass time, for example share photos with distant family and friends as we wander round an overseas city. But even the second, more open type of platform limits what we can do, because it is based on the operations of software which allow computers to interact in particular ways, not others. So you cannot read a book on Facebook, though you could post a video of yourself reading one (not a very interesting video perhaps).

What drives most platforms is the extraction of data about us, the users, that might have potential commercial value. Such data only starts to have value when, through vast calculative power, it can be processed on a very large scale, so that patterns can emerge: patterns, for example, about what distinguishes me as a user of Facebook from you, or what distinguishes those to whom I am connected on Facebook from those to whom you are connected. Let's look in a little more detail at how this works.

Platforms That Track Us

Algorithmic programs exist to find differences, to establish patterns of difference. Those patterns of difference are valuable because, for example, they enable marketers to target their messages more closely (in the industry this is called 'person-alization'). But the change goes much wider. A new language of social description is developing. We are not talking here about the stories that you or I tell about the social world in our own words, but rather about the things that corporate computer programs can count and the patterns that emerge from processing those numbers. For this to happen, the world we live in needs to be *broken down* into things that can be counted: network connections, numbers of friends, numbers of retweets, numbers of times I have performed this transaction or input-ted that data. But the scale of data collection is so great, and its importance to profit so huge, that we can go further and say that the social world itself is being reimagined – through data. Such data is of many sorts, but one important form is data derived from tracking our time on the various online plat-forms that, precisely, encourage us to yield up more data to algorithms for counting.

There are, for sure, some positive consequences of algorithms. Algorithmically curated platforms like Facebook and Twitter give us the chance to act at a large scale, whenever and from wherever we want. We often know movements today by the Twitter hashtag that enabled them to coalesce around a common focus: #Indignados, #Occupy,

#BlackLivesMatter, and #MeToo. It is no exaggeration to say that, algorithmically coordinated, platforms have helped expand our imagination of what sorts of social and civic action are possible.

But there are also costs to the operations of algorithms, and the continuous monitoring of human beings on which they depend. Staying with movements for a moment, mobilization via platforms whose business is to track people, like Facebook and Weibo, exposes movements to more intense surveillance by governments and other forces. The dangers of acting 'in plain sight' are now a key risk that social activists need to deal with. There are plenty of cases where this balance of power turned in favour of political authorities. One example was Mexico's #yosoy132 movement. This movement started in 2012 as a humorous but serious protest against a government minister who had mocked the small size of a demonstration against him: the hashtag means 'I am number 132', that is, the next member to join the demonstration. The hashtag spread like wildfire, and generated an effective challenge to the minister. But the movement was also infiltrated by a government spy who created its website as a means to gather information about movement members for government use.[4]

Over the long term, will algorithmically based

platforms enhance or damage the political opportunities for social movements? We cannot be sure, but it is plausible that the main benefits of continuous data collection about our activities online are likely to accrue to large-scale power: to governments, who can negotiate special access to the vast sea of data that platforms own, but also to the largest players in the media system (Google or Facebook in the West; Alibaba and Tencent in China), who, by continuously monitoring us and harvesting the data that results, gain huge 'surveillance assets'.[5] As citizens are increasingly coming to realize, those assets have real value, and that value is becoming increasingly important in how business runs today.

Data Collection in Everyday Life

What does all this mean? Everyday social life is not normally the sort of activity that is meant to carry risks. Hanging out with friends and family is meant to be just that – relaxed activity, with few, if any, consequences: a time when we can restore our minds and bodies before returning to work. But things are not so simple. Hanging out on Facebook is *not* just hanging out: when using a digital platform, we must comply with its 'terms and conditions', and stay within the environment created by that platform to meet its commercial objectives. Doing so generally means allowing data to be generated about us.

A social media platform like Facebook has colossal reach: nearly 2.3 billion users worldwide.[6] Facebook is concerned not just to gather data from us, but to stimulate our interactions with the platform in ways that will generate more data from ourselves and others. Facebook algorithms do not just track what you do and whom you link with, but versions of what your 'friends' on the platform have posted that Facebook thinks most likely to generate more interactions.

It is not only Facebook that is interested in your data that it gathers: your data has a considerable value to third parties, because it provides almost intimate insights into whom you connect with, and on what terms. For some years, Facebook actively encouraged third parties to access that data through its 'API', or application programming interface. It was this aspect of Facebook's business that it had to adjust in response to the Cambridge Analytica scandal in March 2018.

Have you noticed how you are often asked to access other services via your Facebook login? This is how Facebook helps the marketing industry tie together the data that marketers may have about you, drawn from how you use the web, with the data Facebook holds, generating ever more interesting patterns about you and your connections.

The idea, introduced earlier, of an algorithmic imaginary starts to take shape: a way of imagining you and your potential to generate revenue for corporations. This imaginary is basic to doing business in contemporary capitalism. One development driving this trend is a complete reorganization of marketing and advertising in recent years. Through most of the twentieth century, marketers were limited to mass marketing: the street billboard that a passer-by hopefully noticed; the TV commercial or newspaper ad that a viewer or reader hopefully read; the general online ad that a user hopefully clicked. But now online ads can be targeted very precisely to you at a suitable moment online, on the basis of marketing data previously gathered about you or people very like you. By imagining you differently, marketers are able to target you more precisely.

You might respond that, even so, many ads that reach us online still seem wide of the mark. But targeted advertising is only part of a much wider transformation. Numerous devices are emerging that extract even more data from people's daily life, even when they are not holding computer devices in their hands. Consider digital personal assistants like

Amazon's Echo, whose 'skills' will, Amazon hopes, increase its long-term profitability. How? By gathering continuous streams of data about what you do and want, and by servicing your needs seamlessly.[7] Or consider wearable devices, which gather data about us, our health and fitness, as we train, walk, or just sleep. Some marketers hope that computer chips, embedded beneath the skin, will, before long, perform similar functions.

These trends are particularly important in retail marketing, where the competition for consumer attention is intense. Data gathered via your smartphone can now help marketers target precisely weighted offers direct to your phone at the moment you are approaching a store where the product is on sale. Unless you are careful to switch off the relevant app settings on your phone, your reactions in-store to that offer and anything else may also add to the data gathered. Given the GPS information embedded in your phone and in the products you are near, your phone will be able to pick up how long you spend close to a product. Your phone camera and microphone may even be able to pick up more information about your reaction to the product – all of it useful to marketers.

Imagining

A Corporate Eye on the World

Many commentators are concerned at the new forms of indirect social management that are emerging through these data-driven means. There are two main types of concern.

The first concern is that it has become increasingly normal for corporations to ask for, or demand, the ability to track you as you go about your day. Many insurers, for example, suggest you also install a tracking device in your car (in return for favourable premiums), so that a moment-by-moment record of your driving can be fed straight through to the insurer to influence its assessment of the sort of risk you pose.

The second concern lies with the judgements that this corporate surveillance enables. Sometimes, the data analytics company is not acting for itself, but on hire to some arm of government, for example local government. The lack of funding which plagues local government in most countries provides an obvious incentive to replace human judgement of overwhelming caseloads with what's called 'predictive analytics'. In the UK recently we discovered this was happening with decisions by some social service departments as to whether children should be categorized as 'at risk' or families categorized as 'troubled': data drawn upon and processed by algorithms can include anything from school attendance to rent arrears.[8]

But, and this is crucial to remember, such corporate algorithms really are acts of imagination. There is no space here for technical detail, but let me try to get to the core of the issue. As we saw, algorithms work – they can only work – by counting. The question is what they count. This is as true of algorithms which merely count as it is of algorithms designed to predict what will happen in a precisely defined circumstance, for example whether I will become more loyal to a supplier if a discount is offered to me. The actual world is messy, and does not break down neatly into things that can be counted, while the future world is not there to be counted yet, and so can only be modelled. Algorithmic programs therefore work by constructing what are called 'proxies': workable substitutes for messier features of the actual world in the past or future.

Imagine that a company wants to calculate to whom it should make a loan. In today's world, it is likely to have a vast range of data to draw upon in making that decision, including data bought from other companies. To manage this data, the corporation will want to develop a 'rule of thumb' (or proxy) that can reliably signal from patterns in that mass of data whether someone is the sort of person who is likely to pay back a loan or not. This proxy has to be generated from somewhere. It is generated by using large computing power to establish what also happened with other people in the past who did, or did not, pay back their loans. Through endless repeated computer sequences, the attempt is made to find data patterns that accompanied certain real outcomes (for example, X did, or Y didn't, pay back their loan). When a match is found, this becomes the proxy that gets used to 'predict' future events.

Problems may arise because of the past data used to generate the new proxy. This, in the industry, is called 'training data'. What if that data is skewed, because it has been selected from a set of data that happens to be drawn from a particular slice of the population? If so, the patterns generated by using that training data may be influenced by those historic patterns (say, of class or racial inequality) that shaped the training data. The new algorithm's training will therefore have biases which, when applied, will leave their mark on the world. The result, as a number of data scholars have warned, is likely to be real discriminations against real people.

Deep within corporations that use algorithmic power, whether to drive media platforms or for other types of business, the world is being put together differently. By processing the bits that make up the world in radically new ways, corporations are generating new starting points for their actions in the world: new data, new goals, new targets, new definitions of success. As a result, real human beings, because of the operation of an algorithm, may not receive a loan, access to a social benefit, or a place for their child on an educational programme. What worries critics of these processes is how opaque they are, and how hidden from public view. The more hidden they are, the more likely that new injustices and inequalities will go unchecked.

Conclusion: New Imagination for an Algorithmic Age?

I have been arguing – and the argument may be controversial to some – that something strange is going on with social imagination in the age of large-scale computing power.

For sure, in parts of the traditional media, the imaginative contribution of huge computing power to special visual effects has been astonishing. We could easily have spent this whole chapter discussing how the animation industry has been transformed by CGI. This has reached the point where the leading Hollywood company Framestore now offers, as part of its *pro bono* work, a special bus trip for kids. The bus picks them up in, say, downtown Atlanta, and in a few minutes its windows become computer projection screens. Suddenly the kids seem to be in a bus driving on the surface of Mars – astonishing![9] Meanwhile, other forms of computing power use algorithms to process vast swathes of data collected from our behaviour online. In doing so, deep in corporate backrooms, the world is being imagined in new ways, targeted towards the extraction of profit.

There is a paradox here. Once, the imaginative power of media – for example, the nineteenth-century novel – was used to *reduce* the opacity of the social world: to make its vast complexity more manageable by uncovering patterns. But today the newly unleashed imaginative power of algorithmic processes, working deep within business, is *increasing* the social world's opacity, at least to the human beings on the receiving end of algorithmic decision-making. Perhaps we need a new form of imaginative media – whether film, novel, or computer game – to help us imagine better the consequences of this emerging data-driven world.

This chapter has focused on what media do on a large scale. In the next chapter, we turn to something individual humans have always done on a small scale through media: to share. How do today's media support human beings' love of sharing, for good or ill?

4

Sharing

Earlier chapters have focused on what media do *to* people: connect them to large-scale infrastructures, represent the world back to them, help them imagine the world in new ways. In this chapter, we look at what those outside media institutions (audiences and users) can do *through* media. One of the main things they do through media is to share. Human beings, as social animals, get pleasure from sharing. Media, as technologies for transmitting meaning, have come to seem a natural vehicle for us sharing things. Communication is a key tool for this. After all, the term 'communication' comes from the Latin words for to 'share or make common'.[1]

In this chapter, we think about the contemporary media ecology from a different angle. We explore the role that human sharing has played throughout media's history, particularly via interpersonal media, but also, in certain ways, through mass media. We see how sharing plays a role in the building of social life, via trust, and how today's online platforms constitute an important and distinctive phase in the history of human sharing. But we will also see that, although sharing has clear positive features, it can, under some social conditions, come with harmful consequences too.

Forever Sharing

We tend to think of communication as mutual. People think of themselves as 'in communication' when one person shares information or a story with another in return for the other sharing something back at some point. This is called 'interpersonal communication'. But during the twentieth century, media, the form of communications on which we focus in this book, meant the transmission of meaning in ways that were *not* mutual, *not* interpersonal: so-called '*mass*' media, where the principal role of the 'mass' was simply to receive what was broadcast to them. Interestingly, radio, which we generally think of as a one-way mass medium, was originally a two-way medium until it was reconfigured in the 1910s so that it only worked one-way, outlawing the sharing practices of amateur broadcasters who had been swapping ideas and sounds across the radio waves, but in the process interfered with the profit opportunities of US commercial broadcasters.[2] Mass audiences, however, found ways to share information and reactions around the margins of media: sending newspaper cuttings, recommending novels, telling stories about what they saw on television last night. But those acts of sharing went almost entirely unrecorded.

The progress of mass media in the nineteenth and twentieth centuries has obscured the role of sharing in media history. Interpersonal media (the letter, the telephone) are forms of sharing. The modern phenomenon of mass media 'news' emerged between the sixteenth and eighteenth centuries out of the basic human act of passing on what's new ('new stories'). Early forms of news were gazettes or newsletters, circulated by post or courier, but in large cities like Paris, there might also be walking 'newsmen' or *nouvellistes* who shared snippets of news direct with whoever paid them.

The gradual improvement of postal services helped people share information more widely across space. Letters became the best way of regularly keeping in touch with people who one did not see every day. In the nineteenth century, there were several postal collections and deliveries per day in large cities in Britain. (We can learn about this in the novels of Jane Austen.) Indeed in eighteenth-century Britain there was even a fashion for the 'epistolary' novel, for example Henry Richardson's *Clarissa*, which took the form of letters (or epistles), each letter answering another.

In the early twenty-first century, we have witnessed an explosion of mutual sharing through media. Across the internet, we now share all sorts of things that before it was complicated, even impossible, to share, except face-to-face: photos, media we like, political opinions, anything that amuses us. People and things are connected through media and meaning gets shared through those connections.

We may in future decades look back on media's history in the twentieth century, when mass media became sharply separated from interpersonal communication, as a historical aberration, just a temporary stage in the growth of complex societies. The emergence in the early twenty-first century of the internet as an overarching infrastructure that brings together mass media and interpersonal communication – one-way transmission and mutual sharing – may soon seem the historical norm. Let's pursue this thought by looking at the broader consequences of sharing for social life.

Sharing

Media, Sharing, and the Building of Social Life

Imagine a world where we did *not* share things through 'media'. It would be a world limited to everyday face-to-face interaction in whatever village, town, or city we lived. Today it is really hard to imagine that world functioning without some communication at a distance. Yet in earlier eras, economic activities, for example, occurred largely without any communication in advance, by people simply travelling to another place with whatever they wanted to sell and hoping to find a buyer. That is what markets were: places where people regularly came together from multiple places in the hope of exchanging goods. In the course of meeting, they also shared news of all sorts. Visit a weekly market in many parts of France and you will see this communicational role of markets alive and well.

Sharing things is one way that people build trust between each other. I start to trust you if you share with me some valuable information, or something personally significant to you. You trust me, in return, if I do the same. Once we trust each other a bit, we have the basis for sharing more things – doing more things – together. It follows that media infrastructures which help us share things are important to large societies and their possibilities for forming trust. And trust is one of the main social defences against disorder: when trust is absent, there is an increased risk that human life gets organized by violence rather than through more peaceful means: legal or political process, institutional or community norms.

Mass media, too, are part of this history of sharing at scale. Even if, historically, television and radio only transmitted content one-way, media producers could still rely on people sharing stories about whatever mass media were in circulation. As mass media spread, they enabled even isolated communities to feel part of something larger, a society with a common history and a common present. Mass media, whether the newspaper, the soap opera series, or the one-off TV drama, did much more than just circulate bits of information: they helped in building shared beliefs about society, its problems and opportunities. As US historian of communication James Carey wrote, mass media, through the forms of sharing they encouraged, played a role in 'the maintenance of society in time'.[3]

Sharing, however, can be done well or badly. There is always, as Raymond Williams noted, the question of who gets included in the act of sharing, and who does not: what aspects of life get shared, and what do not.[4] Societies that share badly in this sense (that is, they are uneven in whom they include in their communications) cannot, Williams suggested, be genuinely called democratic. There is a deep insight here that is worth exploring. By sharing meanings, human beings recognize each other as human beings; by contrast, uneven patterns of sharing which leave some voices silent or unrepresented result in people feeling that their society does not represent them. Media, in all their forms, are crucial here. Williams, writing in the 1960s, already saw that media, through how well or badly they share and allow us to share, could shape the health of a society.

Online Sharing: An Expanding Universe

Fast forward to today. Almost everything, it seems, can now be shared online: from the images and sounds of our daily life to the huge data files that record outer space; from our grocery orders, and what they reveal about our wider preferences, to the complex instructions necessary to build an object via a 3D printer.

Whole new genres of sharing have emerged. Blogs which record our daily thoughts, experiences, and tastes are more than a decade old, so we can easily forget how radical a change they represented from the old-style handwritten diary, whose audience was principally the writer's future self. The blog is aimed at an audience of people near and far whom the blogger may only very partly know. It has morphed into other forms: the vlog, the podcast. And these are just some of many new styles of sharing in the digital age. We swap pictures of the food we are eating or the clothes we are wearing, or perhaps even just considering buying. We ping GIFS at each other mashed together from fragments of mass media. Just as with the telephone a century ago, but through a vastly expanded array of media forms, people are sharing things, and on many varied scales.

As with the telephone, those we share with are generally those we already know. But there is one key difference from the era of the telephone's introduction. It seems now much easier to get to know people we have never physically met, owing to the sheer variety and intensity of what we can share through media. You can at least *feel* you know someone by reading online everything they have posted on Twitter or Instagram, or downloading a podcast or YouTube video they've made, or tracking what they like on Spotify.

This gives us a new way of thinking about the contemporary media ecology. Starting from some simple principles – (1) that human beings like to, and need to, share and (2) that, historically, media have generally been technologies for sharing – we can see the internet not just as a huge computing and engineering achievement, but also as a vast space for human sharing on multiple scales. This raises a truly difficult question: whether this vast planetary sharing machine that we call the internet will, over the long term, work for good or ill in the ecology of human life.

There are many directions we could take to pursue this question. As we saw, economic markets have always in part been cultural mechanisms for exchanging information across a territory. Today, as ever more payments move online, new platforms are emerging where this communication function comes, once again, to the fore: take Venmo, a payment app which is also a social media platform, where you are encouraged to share information on your payments with your friends. Rather than economics, however, and because its wider consequences are already starting to become clear, let's concentrate on sharing in the domain of politics.

Sharing for Good or Ill

Today's infrastructures for sharing are wider, deeper, than ever before. Are there implications here, as Raymond Williams suggested, for whether our societies are democratic or authoritarian? We shall see there are.

Online sharing may seem like a simple continuation, even if on a vastly expanded scale, of the media-based sharing of earlier eras (sending letters and packages, speaking by phone). But sharing through media today has a feature which makes it distinctive: it leaves traces. When we go online, we use a computer of some sort. Our acts of sharing are computer-based transactions, recorded digitally, and generally archived for the longer term, not just for our benefit, but for the platform's benefit, to ensure that value can be extracted from the data that lies within them. This is another aspect of the processes of surveillance and tracking we discussed in the previous chapter.

Imagine I share a link to a product with you online. Not only will this act of sharing be available in text form for a considerable time, for you and maybe others to see, but it will also create benefits for entities that are not direct parties to the data involved in the act of sharing. The first of these are the platforms themselves and all the other corporate entities that benefit from the act of sharing, for example marketers whose product is identified in the link I send you. The second are governments. Depending on the politics of the society where that data is hosted (China or the USA, Russia or Germany?), governments may have greater or lesser power to process the traces we leave online for whatever purposes they choose.

The data trail of each act of sharing may be specific content; or it may be the more abstract 'metadata' that describe the *features* of our act of sharing: *who* shared something *with whom*; how many *times* they have shared something together; *where* they were when they did so; and so on. Computer scientists have proved that individuals can be uniquely identified from quite limited metadata about their communications (not even including their name!). Once I have been identified uniquely, even though not named, aspects of my behaviour relative to others can be predicted with alarming accuracy.

Sharing is no longer, therefore, a neutral social act that occurs outside operations of power. Acts of sharing, through the data traces they generate, have become a resource for corporations and governments. Something fundamental is going on here. Merely by sharing things as humans always have done, but in a new online environment set up to monitor us, we are becoming subject to a new form of power. We still think of sharing on a very local scale: I share a story with you, whom I know.

But that is not the most important form of sharing today. First, I may accidentally be sharing data with corporations and governments, although the sharing tends to be one-way: they don't share data back to me about themselves! Second, the nature of the internet as an infrastructure of connection means that I never know whether someone known to me with whom I have shared something will, in turn, share it with someone I don't know. Sometimes I want this to happen, of course, hoping that my smart post will be widely retweeted. But from this basic fact flows the possibility of messages spreading virally across whole populations, linked by the space of connection that is the internet. The speed and scale at which messages and content can spread online had no precedent in the age before the internet.

There is every reason to be worried about what this means for today's societies. Can their social fabric survive the rumour wildfires that internet sharing makes possible? Through transformations in media, a basic feature of human life that seemed morally neutral, or even positive, for social life – sharing – has started unfolding on scales and at speeds that are extremely hard for societies to manage. Our practices of sharing via digital platforms may have generated a new problem for society. Let's consider some examples in the political domain.

Media Sharing and the Seeds of Violence

Accelerated patterns of sharing may generate worries in societies whose political or social cultures are already deeply polarized. So, for example, in the contemporary USA – a society of very deep political and identity divides over race, religion, morality – online sharing is creating a new media culture linked to the so-called 'alt-right'. Some alt-right outlets are well established and well known, such as Breitbart News and Rush Limbaugh's talk show; others are more ephemeral and individual.

As an important recent study from Harvard University discovered, what is distinctive about such alt-right media is not just that they offer an alternative news agenda to the mainstream media, but that they seek to educate their viewers on the irresponsibility of the mainstream media, as a reason to no longer pay attention to it.[5] They may be having success: a recent statistic shows that just over half of US Republican supporters believed that 'the media is the enemy of the people', rather than 'an important part of democracy'.[6] Yet the USA's new right-wing alternative media is based precisely *on sharing*: sharing stories and interpretations of mainstream news stories that are known to be unacceptable in mainstream media. We might call this *exclusive sharing*: sharing that targets a potential in-group, but retains a very clear idea of those whom the message will *not* reach (the outgroup). Exclusive sharing aims to build barriers between groups, not wider solidarity, although of course the small in-group gains in a feeling of solidarity. Exclusive sharing does the very *opposite* of maintain society, yet it, too, is grounded in media's facility for helping us to share. Exclusive sharing is not new, but its new effectiveness derives from the increased effectiveness of the internet as a medium for sharing.

A key medium for exclusive sharing is YouTube, the online video warehouse owned by Google. Recall from Chapter 3 how many of our interactions with media today are shaped by the workings of algorithmic calculation. On a platform like YouTube, the goal of algorithms is not to increase social harmony. (And, you might say, why should it be? Corporations exist to make money.) YouTube's algorithms are targeted to optimize traffic – traffic stimulated by comments and sharing. As a result, provocative material which generates lots of comment and sharing is incentivized. So too is nonprovocative material like cat videos, but no one would pretend they have consequences for politics. Provocative and divisive material potentially does.

Platform owners are aware of this: as the chief executive of Snap, Snapchat's owner, noted in early 2019, '[T]hings that are negative actually spread faster and further than things that are positive.'[7]

The alternative right-wing media 'centre' can be seen as a participatory type of media that opposes the values of mainstream media. It is the latter that has for a century shaped the news agenda of US politics. Many US commentators fear that the growing conflict between mainstream and alt-right media 'centres' is affecting the quality of public debate and public engagement. There are parallel developments in other countries such as Germany where far-right websites are also a major concern.[8] 'Mass' internet platforms, such as YouTube, are organized in a way that enables people to share with large networks that they may not physically meet, but with whom they can certainly share their views. Views can be formed and expressed on that platform that are difficult to express in general social settings.

In a number of large countries, including Brazil, India, and Indonesia, WhatsApp has quickly become the communication mode of choice between individuals and within groups. There are many reasons for this: the automatic encryption of its messages; the ease of including images, sound, and video; its ease for use on a smartphone; or because, unlike

Facebook, WhatsApp content is shared between individuals or groups formed for multiple overlapping purposes. A seemingly non-mass platform like WhatsApp, where groups are built person-by-person, would seem to be protected from the possibility of exclusive sharing running wild. But various incidents in 2018 suggested otherwise.

Think back once more to the Brazilian examples noted in this book's introduction and the fears that the recent presidential election in Brazil was influenced more by what circulated on WhatsApp than by official party broadcasts on television. Although the details are hard to establish, bots can create fake groups by harvesting phone numbers online. If sufficient overlaps exist between the membership of WhatsApp groups, then messages intended originally for particular (real or fake) groups can quickly leap across the divides between groups and spread on a societal scale. When that happens, rumour, gossip, or malice become hard to distinguish from material professionally checked to be safe for wider circulation (that is, news). The result is to produce a dangerous shadow of the journalistic sphere. Similar worries about social media's implications for media and politics exist in other countries, for example Kenya, where WhatsApp is also the most popular social media platform.[9]

Consider what happened in India in July 2018 when videos were widely circulated that appeared to show men taking away young children on motorbikes. Fuelled by those videos, a rumour spread about the existence of a child-kidnapping network, and a number of men were killed by lynch mob on the basis of suspected membership of this non-existent network. These incidents became global news, but they followed a number of less reported incidents in India since 2014.[10] The moral panic that developed around these incidents led the Indian government to accuse WhatsApp of 'abetting' the crimes. WhatsApp's response was interesting. It was to limit the ability to forward messages to more than five people. Initially, this rule was only for Indian phone numbers on WhatsApp. But when Indian groups got round the rule by buying up non-Indian phone numbers, WhatsApp made the rule global.

Think how strange this is. A platform like WhatsApp that was created to make sharing easier feels forced to restrict sharing! Something equally odd happened recently with Pinterest, the platform for saving pictures to virtual pinboards, which is very popular in the USA. Pinterest has become a platform where those opposed to child vaccinations against major diseases spread inflammatory messages. The resulting rise in 'vaccine hesitancy' among mothers in the USA and elsewhere has become so dramatic that the World Health Organization recently called it one of the ten major threats to global health for 2019. What was Pinterest's response? To interfere with the platform's search function, restricting the searchability of material related to vaccination (for *or* against).[11]

What these cases illustrate is that the software-based architecture of today's digital platforms may in contexts of historical conflict become a vital ingredient in the health or toxicity of contemporary societies. Why else would platforms feel the need to interfere with their platforms' basic functions to address a potential social harm?

Put differently, the scale and speed of how we can share content via online platforms – and the degree to which those platforms do, or do not, have built into them 'fire-breaks' that limit sharing – has become a moral, not merely a technological, question. It affects the health of the media ecology that we sustain together. It is certainly not a matter we can just leave to platforms to manage.

Conclusion: Media Sharing and the Architecture of Social Life

'Sharing' is one aspect of an even larger trend. Contemporary media and their design – what we might call the architecture of media platforms and infrastructures – is shaping contemporary societies' tendencies to order or disorder. This problem is structural and it is global.

When media in this way start to affect the basic flow of social (and political) life, its spaces and channels of circulation, its rhythms and bottlenecks, there is no way of ensuring a good outcome. It is as if we asked an architect who had just designed a building to guarantee that the building will always be used for good purposes. She could not. Yet, as with buildings, some media architectures over time become healthy and some become sick; some create incentives for antisocial behaviour, while others create disincentives. We need to become more effective at distinguishing one type of architecture from the other.

We approach here an even larger question: whether societies can be governed *at all* under digital conditions. What if they can't? What would be the implications for the processes of mutual consultation and decision-making that we call democracy? These are questions that we explore in the last chapter.

5

Governing

Media have always had an ambiguous relation to politics. On the one hand, many uses of media have challenged entrenched power (from pamphlet to the community radio station to a brave contemporary whistle-blower like Edward Snowden). From this perspective, media are often pictured as guarantors of freedom, with censorship a clear denial of freedom. On the other hand, governments have often sought to exercise control over media in subtle ways, influencing how media represent them and the wider world. In this final chapter, we look again at this second side of the debate and ask what is media's own role in ensuring (or perhaps hindering) the governability of large societies.

For reasons explored in previous chapters, there are many factors today which complicate our understanding of how governments and media work together. In this chapter, we will look, first, at how the ways in which media connect populations have themselves begun to destabilize media's relation to freedom, implicating them in new possibilities of population control. We will go on to ask how media contribute to the sorts of political rule possible in different places. In considering media's role in how societies are governed, all of the media dimensions previously discussed – connecting, representing, imagining, and sharing – come together. We return here to the question about social order that we asked at the start of the book.

First let's clarify some basic principles.

The Centrality of Media to Politics

Recall our working definition of 'media' as technologies that are able, regularly and reliably, to transmit or preserve meanings across space and time. From this, it follows that introducing media into a territory, or indeed introducing new uses of existing media, changes the flow of meanings in that territory.

What has this to do with politics? Politics, at root, can be understood as struggles over the allocation of scarce resources between people in a particular territory.[1] Those struggles may operate through institutions or through force, but either way, it matters a lot how those struggles and resources are represented (as we saw in Chapter 2). On this basis, media – and changes in media practices and media systems – play an important role within the conditions of political struggle. By the same token, governments who wish to preserve their power must seek to shape how media operate in some way or other.

Many of the key turning points of global political history have been associated with eruptions in media. A key role in the rising sense of rebellion that led to the American Revolution of 1776 was played by 500,000 circulating copies of the pamphlet *Common Sense* signed anonymously 'by an Englishman', later identified as the famed political thinker Thomas Paine. In France, a society without political parties, the chaotic circulation of opinion and gossip via pamphlets, stories, and songs became crucial to the emergence of a social opposition to the French royal court's rule, as it increasingly lost legitimacy in the decades leading up to the French Revolution of 1789.

Moving to the twentieth century, in the Iranian Revolution of 1979, a key role was played by the largely forgotten medium of the cassette tape. From exile in Paris, the emerging leader of the revolution, Ayatollah Khomeini, recorded a series of sermons and calls to bring down the Shah's unpopular regime. These were recorded on cassette, and copies were circulated secretly from France back to Iran, where they were copied many times more. By contrast, in Russia and Eastern Europe in the 1970s and 1980s, it was the *samizdat* alternative press that was the focus of opposition to the weakening Soviet regime and its client governments in Warsaw Pact countries.

All the media for social change discussed so far were circulated *within* the country whose state was being challenged. The collapse of the Soviet Union and Warsaw Pact countries in 1989–90, by contrast, was marked by a new factor: the *cross-border* role played by satellite television, such as CNN, in playing back to home populations the events of those revolutions, most notably the fall of the Berlin Wall in November 1989 – events that were presented very differently on state television.

The political upheavals of 1989 were recent history in the heady years when the closed computer network of the early internet rapidly expanded to become an everyday resource. In the early 1990s, the world wide web, which facilitated searching between connected computers and the pages those computers produced (ever since called 'websites'), emerged at a time of hope for positive political change. The optimism of that time fed into narratives about how online 'connection' would transform the world and our possibilities for freedom.

But there is another way of telling media history. On this view, media, rather than underwriting freedom, provide opportunities for governments looking to establish and entrench their power. Perhaps the most well-known example is the BBC, or British Broadcasting Corporation. The BBC emerged as a commercial organization at the start of radio broadcasting, but quickly acquired a close relationship with the British state. From 1922, it was funded by a form of financing (the 'licence fee') that, when later backed by state legislation, ensured the BBC's formal financial independence from the state. The BBC had a broad remit of national education and entertainment, but a major political crisis (the 1926 General Strike) soon revealed its political role when, notoriously, it allowed itself to be used by government to broadcast anti-strike messages.

The BBC evolved over time into a more inclusive institution. By the 1960s and 1970s, when I was growing up in London, it had a commercially funded rival channel, ITV (Independent Television), yet it had become a national forum for a huge range of entertainment, education, information, and political debate. None of this, however, can disguise the parallel history of the BBC as a bastion of imperial power. When in the 1920s the BBC's first director, Lord Reith, wrote a book-length manifesto for the BBC in an attempt to persuade the British government to recognize it as the official British broadcaster, he wrote of how, through radio's broadcasting power, 'the clock which beats the time over the Houses of Parliament, in the centre of the Empire, is heard echoing in the loneliest cottage in the land'.[2] Over time, the BBC acquired the role of broadcaster to the empire, building the infrastructure that is the basis of today's 'World Service'.

Media, state, and empire became entangled in the history of Britain's then colonies, such as Nigeria and India. There the infrastructure of imperial broadcasting (not just radio, but in Nigeria networks of early cinemas) left a powerful base for subsequent post-colonial governments to build influence over their populations. Throughout the twentieth century, in many countries across the world, anti-colonial struggles involved taking over colonial media and replacing them with new media institutions, very often controlled by the state.

One example was Algeria, where in 1960 the new radio station Voice of Algeria announced to the population their membership of a new independent nation.

A complex example of media's relations with government is the People's Republic of China. Chinese state television, unlike in the UK, was from the start funded by advertising, and so in the 1980s became implicated in complex battles between commercial and state power. The Chinese state's news agency, Xinhua, dates from the 1930s, when the Communist Party had not yet won power, but it has since developed into a major world force, providing international news that reflects the distinctive priorities of the Chinese government. China had joined the long history of states using their news agencies to shape their nation's global profile; also important have been Reuters for the UK and AFP/Agence-France-Presse for France.

Media as Freedom and Control: A Dialectic
We can think of this complicated double history – media's role in supporting both freedom and government power or control – as what social theorists call a 'dialectic': an ever-shifting balance between two historical forces (literally the word means 'conversation'). Without that dialectic – without

the continuous 'conversation' between forces of freedom and control – media, and governing, would get out of balance.

A key argument here has been made by development economist Amartya Sen. Without media's ability to spread news of emerging disasters or crises, governments would simply act in their own interest, and ignore or cover up problems such as food supply or drought. That, rather than an actual lack of food, Sen argues, is very often why famines happen. The pressure of media attention can short-circuit the natural tendency of governments to hide their failures and provide a channel through which solutions can be found before a food crisis develops. For this reason, Sen claims, healthy media institutions are an essential pre-condition of human development.

What stage of this dialectic between media and government have we reached as we approach the third decade of the twenty-first century? For a century or more, in countries of the 'West', there has been a standard answer: that free media institutions (often called, for simplicity, the 'free press'), and the social life that underpins a free press, are sufficient conditions for the broader freedom of the citizens of democratic societies.

But what if freedom for media institutions is no

longer the guarantor of social freedom? What if the first freedom starts to disturb the second? Could it be, as the preceding chapters have suggested, that the extraordinary expansion of social connectedness through media, including, but not limited to, social media platforms, has created new opportunities for states *and* corporations to govern societies in a deeper, more intimate, and less accountable way?

This is certainly not the first time in history when powerful governments have dreamed of synergies between media technologies and the possibilities for greater population control. In the early days of film and radio, the Nazi government in Germany used these national media to instruct a large population in new ways of living and obeying. Joseph Goebbels, the Nazi Minister of Propaganda, used the coverage of Adolf Hitler's vast rallies and the new ability to broadcast the German leader's voice live into every home in the land as a way of training the population in an agenda of radical social change. The fear of speaking out against the new politics led one sociologist who lived through that time to invent a new concept: the spiral of silence. In a spiral of silence, my incentives to speak out against what everyone around me is saying fall steadily, until the point where I say nothing.[3]

Today the media freedom/government dialectic is at an interesting turning point. Consider the contrasting, but also partly overlapping, situations of media in the USA and China. The Chinese government sees the growth of artificial intelligence and a system of social connection underpinned by highly sophisticated digital platforms as 'a market improvement of the social and economic order'.[4] That phrase is taken from the policy document that set out the planning for China's proposed 'social credit system', which aims to score every Chinese citizen for their social behaviour, monitoring them online and rewarding or punishing them for good or bad behaviour. China has the official goal of leading the world in artificial intelligence by 2030: hardly surprising, when this system will depend on algorithms to process the data on people's behaviour. Meanwhile the President of the United States of America, supposedly the opposite pole of China in terms of political freedom, regularly brands the media as 'the enemy of the people', although he has not sought yet to move against media institutions' freedoms.

Which of these relations between state and media points to the future? The overlap between them is, to say the least, disturbing. Where are more traditional visions of media freedom in all this?

Governing

Media and the Future of Political Order

To unravel these questions, it helps to move beyond any naïve idea that freedom is simply opposed to order. Freedom always involves constraints of some sort: my freedom depends on your accepting constraints on acting to undermine my freedom, and vice versa. On a larger scale, the goal of optimizing freedom for millions of people is impossible without multiple levels of restriction through law and other means, restrictions on each of us doing exactly what we like. The point goes beyond personal restrictions, and includes the sorts of institutional and practical order on which a tolerable daily life is built. Our lives cannot be, or feel, free without a certain degree of regularity (the flow of drinking and washing water, electricity, food, medicines, and information). That regularity requires a certain order, and behind it, a degree of control, to be in place.

At a time of rapid change to media and other social institutions, the difficult question is: what is media's role in making a social order that is healthy for freedom?

Today's new means of connection – our extraordinary new capacities to share meanings with those both near and far – appear to be expanding human freedom. This was certainly the dream of the devel-

110

opers and advocates of the internet. The slogan that information 'simply wants to be free' (attributed, but out of context, to the late John Perry Barlow, lyricist for The Grateful Dead) is well known. But what matters more, surely, are media's consequences for the freedom of human beings. Let's consider some of the problems that follow when our freedom to share meanings and information through media becomes unconstrained, problems that have only become apparent in recent years.

First, the power to share news is a freedom enjoyed not just by people but also by automated entities ('bots'). Bots operate within parameters set by human beings, for example political parties or governments, and 'speak' like human beings. Such bots are often used to spread malicious or misleading information. Whether malicious or not, bots are *not* the sort of entity that is entitled to freedom; they are automated programs at the service of other living agents, perhaps even at the service of other software programs! Under great pressure from governments and broader society, therefore, platforms have developed ways of distinguishing bots from human users of their infrastructures and then removing them.

You do not, however, need bots to spread malicious material. Human beings are perfectly capable of doing so. In times of political conflict, one person's malice may be another person's passionate principle. Once again, platforms have come under pressure to introduce more order into their spaces of communication. An important recent example is the banning from Facebook, Twitter, and many other platforms of US extreme right-wing fantasist Alex Jones. In 2018, Jones capped earlier rants by denying the reality of the grief of parents whose kids were killed in recent US school massacres, claiming the whole thing was a hoax and that the parents were being played by actors. It is hard to imagine comments more offensive. The resulting ban was surely justified: voices that don't act as if they are accountable to facts are not voices that deserve protection.

Meanwhile group circulation of messages generates difficult problems for platforms, as we saw in Chapter 4. People may think they can trust what those in their WhatsApp group share – the relaxed context of WhatsApp use encourages this belief – but it is just this belief that makes the service such a powerful, even dangerous, tool in the hands of unscrupulous political actors.

A third problem is not insufficient order in platforms' information flows, but the wrong sort of order. We have seen over the past two chapters that algorithms are increasingly shaping how we imagine the social world. Our imagination of the world that social media platforms present to us is itself shaped by platforms' algorithmic curation of what appears to us there. Algorithms determine what comes top of our feed, and what is never seen at all and so remains in shadow. Facebook posts by 'friends' whose posts we rarely look at are likely to be weighted low by the algorithms that determine what appears in our newsfeed; the posts of those we actively follow will appear high. Getting back to those low-rated posts is difficult (we have to look specifically for them and may not have the time or be prompted to do so). But our sense of what and where social life is happening will be determined by what *appears to us* in the everyday flow, not what lies in the shadow. Yet the algorithmic mechanisms which determine what appears to us are largely opaque. The result is that the social world itself becomes less transparent.

Could it be that platforms' commercial goals of maximizing traffic and interactions for data profit here conflict with wider social, and even political, goals? The issue of representation and the responsibility of those who circulate representations is as old as media, as we saw in Chapter 2. But it takes on a complex new form in societies which rely on corporations to present to us the world of everyday social interaction. Fundamental new issues of trust and responsibility arise. Is it time to question the idea that corporations are capable of taking responsibility for curating our social lives? That, after all, was not what they were set up to do.

In all previous eras, social life included contexts (families, our friend networks, institutions) where what we saw in front of us was not all that was going on. Appearances can always be managed by human beings, but we make allowances for that. The automated algorithmic management of social appearances by platforms such as Facebook presents completely new challenges. What does it mean for a corporation to 'present' all of social life responsibly to those who live it? Why should any entity have the power to do this? What would count as legitimate ways of doing this? How much of this can we safely leave to algorithms and to automation? It may take a whole generation to find the answers to these difficult questions.

Conclusion: Rule by Tweet or Rule by Surveillance?

There is a more direct way of thinking about what media mean for the governability of societies.

Today's world is once again becoming bi-polar, with conflicts over trade and other matters reviving between the USA and China. One key area of trade and competition is artificial intelligence, the tool that drives what can appear to us as social life on digital platforms. Alongside the economic conflict, a different type of clash is emerging between the Chinese and the US styles of governing through media, both of which are deeply problematic.

I have noted at various points the Chinese government's plan to build a more intensely regulated society and economy in which the possibilities for surveillance, inherent in social media and other online platforms, are optimized not to produce freedom, but to ensure order. This would be a model of 'rule by surveillance' that does not fit with any concept of freedom ever developed.

At the same time, right now in the USA, we have an experiment with a form of rule, nominally democratic, that has more than an echo of older forms of royalty. I am referring to the current US President Donald Trump's penchant for announcing policies, making decisions, and effecting appointments or sackings via Twitter.

No one believes in the royalty of President Trump! What is curious, however, is that, since he took office, the world's press have been treating him, in one crucial respect, *as if* he were royal. They have done so by reporting his tweets (which, at the outset, were the passing thoughts of a single man, albeit the most powerful man in the world) as news. By doing so, the press conferred on those tweets exactly the force that Trump claimed for them: the force not of mere thoughts or opinions, but of actual *acts of power*. This is the type of embodied power – to condemn or elevate a person by the movement of a finger (here one that presses 'send') – that was accorded to kings of earlier periods. No wonder the political editor of the UK's *Sun* newspaper commented on his interview with Trump mid-2018 that 'it's like dealing with a medieval king'.[5]

Note the shift here. The brilliance of Trump's move lies in its simplicity: the capacity of Twitter *to connect* large audiences, so that individuals can 'broadcast' directly to unseen others, morphs into the capacity of the already powerful *to rule* by tweet. This is rule outside the constraints that normally shape how policy gets made by a democratic government. So Trump, it seems, announced the withdrawal of US troops from Syria in December 2018 on Twitter without full consultation with his military or governmental colleagues.

Both these contemporary models for rule lie a long way from the historic legacy of democratic government, with all its weaknesses and virtues. And yet both models are based in the very same media infrastructure, an infrastructure that enables both rule by surveillance and rule by tweet.

In the face of these developments, who would doubt that, to understand the challenges, opportunities, and dangers of government in the twenty-first century, we must take seriously the role of media?

Conclusion

Media are technologies for the transmission and storage of symbols, but as we have seen in this book, they are also much more: media contents; the institutions that produce them; the audiences that interpret them; and media's wider circulation in daily life. Put another way, if we are to think about media, we must think about how media operate *in society*. Even so, it might seem surprising that a book called *Media: Why It Matters* has focused so much on the organization of life, rather than, say, the ownership of media corporations or the design of media formats. There is no question that those matters are important, but my emphasis in this book is focused quite deliberately on a different sort of question: the implications that contemporary media have for the forms of human life, government, and society that are possible today.

Conclusion

The value of this broader approach becomes especially clear when we shift from a traditional definition of mass media (the press, radio, television, and film) to consider our uses of the internet in all its myriad forms. And it becomes clear beyond doubt once we consider the deeper levels of symbolic work (and imagination) that make the internet possible: I mean the everyday operations of computers, the data they generate and process, and the vast interconnected infrastructures of algorithmic counting and data processing that help make our media devices function as they do.

The increasing vastness of the term 'media' is the result not of researchers' desire to expand their subject, but of how the world really has become more interconnected and interdependent. Media, as infrastructures of connection, have been the means for this.

We have moved, in the course of this book, from reflecting on particular bits of media content (a novel, a film, an article, a tweet) to thinking about media as *ecologies* of communication through which human life is sustained. Once we begin to reflect on media at that larger scale, we realize how complex and ambivalent are the consequences of media for the worlds in which we live. Ask how well media contribute to politics or the sustaining of orderly government, as we did in Chapter 5, and the discussion becomes even more uncertain.

There is today a sense of crisis about media. There are more and less useful ways of interpreting this crisis. We can see it as the steady unravelling of older media structures and forms, but this risks assuming as our reference point a 'golden age' of media which never existed: the nineteenth century, after all, had its 'yellow press', the US's rabid equivalent of today's tabloid newspapers, while large parts of the twentieth-century audience did not feel mass broadcasting represented them fairly, or perhaps even at all.

It is better to see the contemporary problems discussed in this book as the result of the success of media as much as of their failure. It is because of the extraordinarily fast expansion in the past three decades of social interconnection through the internet, and because of the proliferation of countless new forms for making and circulating media, that ecological questions of online politics and social civility have become so urgent.

This might, in the end, be what studying media means: taking seriously in all their complexity the environmental implications of the infrastructures of connection (media) that human beings have built over the past three centuries. Thinking seriously about how we might need to *live differently* within today's media ecologies in order that we and future generations have a better life. Such an understanding of media, and how they work, or fail to work, is no luxury, but a basic faculty that all human beings need today.

There are, of course, many other topics on which this book could have focused: the threat of cyberwar and the broader security issues that the internet, as currently organized, raises; the consequences for our physical environment of the pollution that defunct media devices create and all the other environmental costs of our media consumption; the consequences of media for the economy (from automated algorithmically driven trading on the stock exchange to the new economic relations involved in digital platforms); the consequences for the economic viability of journalism when the advertising that has largely cross-subsidized it for two centuries is undergoing a data-driven revolution; or, finally, the fundamental role that media have played in the eruption of this decade's intensifying gender politics.

I hope, however, through this short book's emphasis on media's implications for the fabric of social life, to have given you, whatever your interests, a better sense of why media matters. Whatever your specialism, it matters to have some understanding of how media work and the difference they make to the worlds we share.

There is, for sure, no point in studying media to the exclusion of everything else, when it is broader questions about the quality of our lives together that drive us to be interested in media in the first place. But equally, to study other domains – whether economics, politics, or even biology – as if media didn't matter would be to go blind into today's world. We live in a world where not only do media matter, but they shape our world, and its possibilities for order and disorder, in ways that we must try to grasp before it is too late.

Notes

Introduction

1 Paulo Freire, *The Politics of Education* (New York: Bergin & Garvey, 1985), 3.

2 Michael Fox, 'The Brazilian Truckers' Strike: How WhatsApp is Changing the Rules of the Game', *Truthout*, 15 June 2018, *https://truthout.org/articles/the-brazilian-truckers-strike-how-whatsapp-is-changing-the-rules-of-the-game/*; Caio Machado and Marco Konopacki, 'Computational Power: Automated Use of WhatsApp in the Elections', *ITS Rio*, 26 October 2018, *https://feed.itsrio.org/computational-power-automated-use-of-whatsapp-in-the-elections-59f62b857033*.

3 Dave Cullen, 'Changing the Story', *Guardian*, 9 February 2019.

Chapter 1 Connecting

1 *https://www.gsmaintelligence.com/*.

2 Latin *fanaticus*, derived from *fanum*, meaning a place holy to a god.

3 'WhatsApp: the Widespread Use in Political Campaigning in the Global South', July 2018, *https://ourdataourselves.tacticaltech.org/posts/whatsapp/*.

4 Laura Cappon, 'Egypt's Struggle for Freedom Goes Online', *The New Arab*, 11 February 2018, *https://www.alaraby.co.uk/english/indepth/2018/2/11/egypts-struggle-for-freedom-goes-online*.

5 Fergus Millar quoted in Claudia Moatti, 'Translation, Migration and Communication in the Roman Empire: Three Aspects of Movement in History', *Journal of Classical Antiquity* 25(1) (2006): 109–40, at 128.

6 Michael Clanchy, *From Memory to Written Record: England 1066–1307* (Oxford: Blackwell, 1993).

7 *https://www.huffpost.com/entry/google-ceo-on-privacy-if_n_383105*.

8 Claude Fischer, *America Calling* (Berkeley: University of California Press, 1992).

9 Leo Tolstoy, *Anna Karenina* (Harmondsworth: Penguin, 1954), 3 (originally published 1873).

10 See *http://www.who.int/substance_abuse/activities/addictive_behaviours/en/*.

11 Manuel Castells, *Communication Power* (Oxford: Oxford University Press, 2009), 55.

12 Justin McCurry and Nemo Kim, 'South Korea is Forced to Act Against Spycam Sex Snoopers', *Guardian*, 3 July 2018.

Chapter 2 Representing

1 Stuart Hall, 'Encoding/Decoding', in Center for Contemporary Cultural Studies, *Culture, Media Language* (London: Hutchinson, 1980), 128–38. For the original version of the paper, see *https:// www.birmingham.ac.uk/Documents/college-arts law/history/cccs/stencilled-occasional-papers/1to8 and11to24and38to48/SOP07.pdf*. Some argue that Hall's insights were anticipated by 1950s US research, but this point remains controversial. For the debate, see James Curran, *Media Power* (London: Routledge, 2002), 116–22; David Morley, 'Active Audience Theory: Pendulum and Pitfalls', *Journal of Communication*, 43(4) (1993): 13–19.

2 Walter Benjamin, *Illuminations* (New York: Schocken Books, 1968), 240; Don DeLillo, *White Noise* (London: Picador, 1985), 184.

3 Ofcom, *Children and Parents: Media Use and Attitudes Report Executive Summary* (2019), 5, *https://www.ofcom.org.uk/__data/assets/pdf_file/00 24/134907/Children-and-Parents-Media-Use-and-Attitudes-2018.pdf*.

4 Michał Krzyżanowski and Per Ledin, 'Uncivility on the Web: Populism in/and the Borderline Discourses of Exclusion', *Journal of Language and Politics*, 16(4) (2017): 566–81.

5 Nicholas Negroponte, *Being Digital* (Cambridge, MA: MIT Press, 1995).

6 Emily Bell, 'Facebook Creates Orwellian Headache as News is Labelled Politics', *Guardian*, 24 June 2018.

7 Pierre Bourdieu, *Language and Symbolic Power* (Cambridge: Polity, 1991), 166.

Chapter 3 Imagining

1 Quotes from Honoré de Balzac, *Old Goriot* (Harmondsworth: Penguin, 1951), 37–8, 28.
2 Exceptions include Ken Loach's film *It's a Free World* (2007), about Polish migrants in London, the Dardenne brothers' films *Lorna's Silence* (2008) and *The Unknown Girl* (2016), and Costa Gavras's *Eden is West* (2009).
3 Raymond Williams, 'Drama in a Dramatized Society' (1974), republished in Jim McGuigan (ed.), *Raymond Williams on Culture and Society: Essential Writings* (Thousand Oaks, CA: Sage, 2014), 161–71, at 165.
4 Emiliano Treré, 'The Struggle Within: Discord, Conflict and Paranoia in Social Movement Protest', in Lina Dencik and Oliver Leistert (eds), *Critical Perspectives on Social Media and Protest* (Lanham, MD: Rowman & Littlefield, 2015), 163–80.
5 Shoshana Zuboff, *The Age of Surveillance Capitalism* (London: Profile Books, 2019), 94.
6 At least according to Facebook's own statistics, as reported by *https://www.statista.com* (2018, third quarter).
7 Laura Stevens, 'Amazon Wants Alexa to do More Than Just Play Your Music', *Wall Street Journal*, 20 October 2018.
8 Niamh MacIntyre and David Pegg, 'Councils Use

377,000 People's data in Efforts to Predict Child Abuse', *Guardian*, 16 September 2018.

9 *https://www.framestore.com/fieldtriptomars.*

Chapter 4 Sharing

1 Raymond Williams, *Keywords* (London: Fontana, 1983), 72.

2 Eric Barnouw, *Tube of Plenty* (New York: Oxford University Press, 1990).

3 James Carey, *Communication as Culture* (London: Routledge, 1983), 18.

4 This is the underlying argument of Raymond Williams's great book *The Long Revolution* (Harmondsworth: Penguin, 1961).

5 Yochai Benkler, Rob Faris, and Hal Roberts, *Network Propaganda* (Oxford: Oxford University Press, 2018).

6 Poll by Qunnipiac University, April 2018, detailed results at *https://poll.qu.edu/search-releases/search-results/release-detail?What=&strArea=6;0;&strTime=28&ReleaseID=2539#Question001.*

7 Quoted in Mike Isaac, 'Facebook's Mark Zuckerberg Says He'll Shift Focus to Users' Privacy', *New York Times*, 6 March 2019.

8 Guy Chazan, 'Websites Burst "Liberal Bubble" of Germany's Old-Style Media', *Financial Times*, 10 September 2018.

9 Nanjala Nyabole, *Digital Democracy, Analogue Politics: How the Internet Era is Transforming Politics in Kenya* (London: Zed Books, 2019).

10 'Officials Blame WhatsApp for Spike in Mob Killings, but Indians Say Vicious Party Politics are at Fault', Global Voices, 2 August 2018, *https://globalvoices. org/2018/08/02/officials-blame-whatsapp-for-spike-in-mob-killings-but-indians-say-vicious-party-poli tics-are-at-fault/*; Aria Thaker, 'WhatsApp is Going Global with a Restriction Used to Fight Fake News in India', *Quartz India*, 22 January 2019, *https:// qz.com/india/1529461/whatsapp=indian=step-agai nst-fake-news-has-gone-global/*.

11 Christina Caron, 'Pinterest Restricts Vaccine Search Results to Prevent Spread of Misinformation', *New York Times*, 26 February 2019.

Chapter 5 Governing

1 I am drawing here on a 1960s definition of politics as 'the authoritative allocation of goods, services, and values': David Easton, *A Systems Analysis of Political Life* (New York: John Wiley, 1965). This definition remains useful, provided we remember the symbolic struggle that such 'allocation' always involves.

2 John Reith, *Broadcast over Britain* (London: Hodder & Stoughton, 1924), 220.

3 Elizabeth Noelle-Neuman, 'The Spiral of Silence: A Theory of Public Opinion', *Journal of Communication*, 24 (1974): 43–51.

4 'Planning Outline for the Construction of a Social Credit System (2014–2020)', *https://chinacopy rightandmedia.wordpress.com/2014/06/14/ planning-outline-for-the-construction-of-a-social-*

credit-system-2014-2020/ (translated by Rogier Creemers).

5 Tom Newton-Dunn, interviewed on BBC Radio 4's *Today* programme, 13 July 2018.

Further Reading

Introduction

Communication double bind: Gregory Bateson, *Mind and Nature* (London: Fontana/Collins, 1980), 128–9.

Media industries and their economics: David Hesmondhalgh, *The Cultural Industries* (Newbury Park, CA: Sage, 4th edition, 2018).

Chapter 1

History of printing: Elizabeth Eisenstein, *The Printing Press as an Agent of Change* (Cambridge: Cambridge University Press, 1982); Tsuen-Hsuin Tsien, *Paper and Printing*, volume 5 of Joseph Needham (ed.), *Science and Civilization in China* (Cambridge: Cambridge University Press, 1985).

Marconi: Marc Raboy, *Marconi: The Man Who Networked the World* (Oxford University Press, 2016), especially chapters 20 and 31.

Further Reading

Fan connections: Nancy Baym, *Playing to the Crowd* (New York: New York University Press, 2018).

China's internet policy: China Copyright and Media, 'State Council Guiding Opinions Concerning Vigorously Moving Forward the "Internet Plus" Plan', *https://chinacopyrightandmedia.wordpress.com/2015/07/01/state-council-guiding-opinions-concerning-vigorously-moving-forward-the-internet-plus-plan/* (translated by Rogier Creemers).

Migration and media use: Mirca Madianou and Daniel Miller, *Migration and New Media* (London: Routledge, 2011).

Chapter 2

Work in media, especially news: Mark Deuze, *Media Work* (Cambridge: Polity, 2007); Natalie Fenton (ed.), *New Media, Old News* (Cambridge: Polity, 2009); Pablo Boczkowski and Chris Anderson (eds), *Remaking the News* (Cambridge, MA: MIT Press, 2017).

Social basis of democratic politics: Jean-Jacques Rousseau, *The Social Contract and Discourses* (London: Everyman Library, 1793) (*The Social Contract* was originally published in 1762); Edmund Burke, *Reflections on the Revolution in France* (Oxford: Oxford University Press, 1993) (originally published in 1790).

Media and the modern nation: Benedict Anderson, *Imagined Communities* (London: Verso, 1983).

Further Reading

Media representations of migrants: Myria Georgiou, 'Does the Subaltern Speak? Migrant Voices in Digital Europe', *Popular Communication*, 16(1) (2018): 45–57.

Battles for voice in media: (for the press) James Curran and Jean Seaton, *Power without Responsibility* (London: Routledge, 8th edition, 2018); (for reality TV) Angela McRobbie, 'Notes on "What Not to Wear" and Post-feminist Symbolic Violence', *Sociological Review*, 52(2) (2004): 97–109; and Helen Wood and Beverley Skeggs (eds), *Reality Television and Class* (London: Palgrave Macmillan/BFI, 2011).

Media in the French Revolution: Robert Darnton, 'An Early Information Society: News and Media in Eighteenth-Century Paris', *American Historical Review*, 105(1) (2000): 1–35.

Search engines and race: Safiya Umoja Noble, *Algorithms of Oppression* (New York: New York University Press, 2018).

Social media and news values: Mike Ananny, *Networked Press Freedom* (Cambridge, MA: MIT Press, 2018).

Advertising's changing relations to journalism: Joseph Turow, *The Daily You* (New Haven: Yale University Press, 2012).

Further Reading

Chapter 3

TV drama and society: Raymond Williams, 'Drama in a Dramatized Society' (1974), republished in Jim McGuigan (ed.), *Raymond Williams on Culture and Society: Essential Writings* (Thousand Oaks, CA: Sage, 2014), 161–71.

Algorithms and imagination: Taina Bucher, 'The Algorithmic Imaginary: Exploring the Ordinary Affects of Facebook Algorithms', *Information Communication and Society* 20(1) (2017): 30–44.

Platforms and their social responsibility: Tarleton Gillespie, *Custodians of the Internet* (New Haven: Yale University Press, 2018); Siva Vaidhyanathan, *Anti-social Media* (Oxford: Oxford University Press, 2018).

Mexico's #yosoy132 movement: Emiliano Treré, 'The Struggle Within: Discord, Conflict and Paranoia in Social Movement Protest', in Lina Dencik and Oliver Leistert (eds), *Critical Perspectives on Social Media and Protest* (Lanham, MD: Rowman & Littlefield, 2015), 163–80.

General perspectives on algorithms, data, and capitalism: Nick Couldry and Ulises Mejias, *The Costs of Connection* (Stanford: Stanford University Press, 2019); Shoshana Zuboff, *The Age of Surveillance Capitalism* (London: Profile Books, 2019).

Further Reading

Surveillance generally: David Lyon, *Surveillance After Snowden* (Cambridge: Polity, 2015). And, *if you can*, get hold of a copy of Oscar Gandy's extraordinary 1993 book *The Panoptic Sort: A Political Economy of Personal Information* (Boulder, CO: Westview Press), which saw the surveillance economy coming, but which is now scandalously out of print.

Surveillance by the retail industry: Joseph Turow, *The Aisles Have Eyes* (New Haven: Yale University Press, 2018).

Algorithms and social discrimination: Cathy O'Neil, *Weapons of Math Destruction* (London: Allen Lane, 2016); Virginia Eubanks, *Automating Inequality* (New York: St Martin's Press, 2018). Meredith Broussard, *Artificial Unintelligence* (Cambridge, MA: MIT Press, 2018) offers a detailed explanation of how 'machine learning' works and how biases can unwittingly arise.

Chapter 4

Early history of news: Terhi Rantanen, *When News was New* (Malden, MA: Blackwell, 2009).

Classic texts on the relations between culture and democracy: (for the UK) Raymond Williams, *Culture and Society* (Harmondsworth: Penguin, 1958); (for the USA) James Carey, *Communication as Culture* (London: Routledge, 1983); (for Latin America) Jesús Martín-Barbero, *Communication Culture and Hegemony: From the Media to Mediations* (Newbury Park, CA: Sage, 1993).

Sharing online: Nicholas A. John, *The Age of Sharing* (Cambridge: Polity, 2016). See also more generally Lee Humphreys, *The Qualified Self: Social Media and the Accounting of Everyday Life* (Cambridge, MA: MIT Press, 2018).

Social media, US democracy, and right-wing extremism: Yochai Benkler, Rob Faris, and Hal Roberts, *Network Propaganda* (New York: Oxford University Press, 2018); Rebecca Lewis, 'Alternative Influence: Broadcasting the Reactionary Right on YouTube', *Data and Society*, 18 September 2018, *https://datasociety.net/output/alterna tive-influence/* .

Chapter 5

Media and the Iranian Revolution: Anabelle Sreberny Mohammadi and Ali Mohammadi, *Small Media, Big Revolution* (Minneapolis: University of Minnesota Press, 1994).

Post-colonial perspectives on media history: (on Nigeria) Brian Larkin, *Signal and Noise* (Durham, NC: Duke University Press, 2008); (on India) Arvind Rajagopal, *Politics After Television* (Cambridge: Cambridge University Press, 2001); (on Algeria) Frantz Fanon, *Studies in a Dying Colonialism* (New York: Monthly Review Press, 1965).

Further Reading

Media and the Chinese state: Yue-Zhi Zhao, *Communication in China* (Lanham, MD: Rowman & Littlefield, 2008).

Media's role in economic development: Amartya Sen, *Development as Freedom* (Oxford: Oxford University Press, 1999).

Media and social progress: I jointly led with Clemencia Rodriguez Chapter 13 (Media and Communications) of the report of the International Panel for Social Progress (*www.ipsp.org/*), which is available from *https://repository.upenn.edu/cargc_strategicdocuments/1/*. The whole twenty-two-chapter report is *Rethinking Society for the XXI Century. Report of the International Panel for Social Progress* (Cambridge: Cambridge University Press, 2018).

Nazism and media: Ian Kershaw (1987) *The Hitler Myth* (Oxford: Clarendon Press, 1987).

Chinese social credit system: China Copyright and Media, 'Planning Outline for the Construction of a Social Credit System (2014–2020)', *https://chinacopyrightandmedia.wordpress.com/2014/06/14/planning-outline-for-the-construction-of-a-social-credit-system-2014-2020/* (translated by Rogier Creemers). (The chapter's quotation is taken from here.)

Twitter and Facebook's algorithmic presentation of news: Zeynep Tufecki, *Twitter and Tear Gas* (New Haven: Yale University Press, 2017).

136

Further Reading

Conclusion

Internet security/insecurity: Bruce Schneier, *Click Here to Kill Everybody* (New York: W.W. Norton, 2018).

Environmental damage from media: Rick Maxwell and Toby Miller, *Greening the Media* (New York: Oxford University Press, 2012).

The platform economy: Nick Srnicek, *Platform Capitalism* (Cambridge: Polity, 2017); Julie Cohen, *Between Truth and Power* (New York: Oxford University Press, 2019), especially Part One.

Digital advertising and the decline of journalism: Joseph Turow, *The Daily You* (New Haven: Yale University Press, 2013).

Digital media and gender politics: Sarah Banet-Weiser, *Empowered: Popular Feminism and Popular Misogyny* (Durham, NC: Duke University Press, 2018).